Even Doctors Have Heart Attacks

CONRAD CASTELLINO MD

Dear Dr. Beckman,
this is my 1st book.
excuse the many mistakes, a
learning curve in operation
Yes it is a real autobiographi-
cal account.

You Student

Conrad

ISBN: 0692016783
ISBN 13: 9780692016787

Library of Congress Control Number: 2012905640
Conrad Castellino
Merced, CA

Contents

Acknowledgements

To a fellow traveler from Kentucky to San Francisco, a chap with a service dog, a beautiful lab, who told me to stop talking and start writing and "let your thoughts free." On that flight, I started to write what I had mulled over for three years. Once I started, it took me three months to pen my thoughts down.

To Manuel, the techie who gave me the skills to do what I should have done two years ago..

To my wife, Doreen, who has put up with me through bad times and even worse times. She has wings sprouting from her shoulders.

To Wayne, my eldest, who read and reread many chapters with me, helping with the occasional blocks that otherwise would have slowed me down and derailed my project.

To Stephen, my brother, and Collette, who read many chapters. Their input was valuable in organizing my thoughts and putting it all down on paper.

TO my physicians Mani, Patel, Trumbull, Daulat and Vik. I would not be here if it were not for you'll. More than physicians I know you'll as good friends. I deeply appreciate all the help and support I received through very trying times. May The good Lord Always smile down upon us all.

Special Recognition

To my high school, Saint Patrick's High School, in Karachi, Pakistan. To the principal, the Rev. Tony Lobo, who saw I had writing skills and gave me much encouragement in all my endeavors. He believed in me, and his words still give me much encouragement. He knew me better than I knew myself, and set the bar very high for me and many others. He has since retired from his position of school principal and now resides in Islamabad, Pakistan, where he holds the title of Bishop Emeritus.

Author Biography

I was born and raised in Pakistan in a close Catholic family. I attended Dow Medical College where I received my bachelor's degrees in medicine and surgery and London University in England for my premed certification. I came to the United States in the 1980s and completed my internship at Providence Hospital in Washington, D.C. In New York, I completed my residency in internal medicine and served as chief resident as a teacher and mentor. I started an internal medicine practice near my family in California and have operated this practice for over eighteen years. I have been a mentor for pre-med students and a volunteer lecturer to nursing students.

I married my soul mate from college, Doreen, and we have two sons. After a near fatal heart attack, I was told that I would not work again. However, my life is as productive now as ever. I continue to share my personal medical history to further inspire others about the possibilities that a medical crisis can bring to their lives.

1

PROLOGUE

I was enjoying my wife's female persuasions on a wonderful Tuesday night, but I might have wished to be excused if I had known what was to follow. We had enjoyed an extended period of intimacy. My heart rate had picked up, it was violently contracting in my chest; my muscles were tense and no doubt driving up my blood pressure; my lungs were sucking in gasps of air, yet the oxygen level in my blood would have dropped with all the activity. My mind knew of nothing other than what was consuming it. My metabolic rate had gone up rapidly and was consuming nutrients. Ahh, the vixen knew what she was doing. However, this was going to be the most expensive experience I had ever had and not just of the monetary kind.

The day was usual in its character, a regular workday, if any day could be called regular. I completed minor physical activities that afternoon with no untoward discomfort or shortness of breath.

At home that evening I did some early spring yard work with weak sun rays warming my back. Being more invigorated than usual, I even made an attempt at a barbecue that was otherwise mediocre, but the Pakistani curry that my wife ad-libbed rescued the meal. The computer on my lap, cell phone by my side, TV playing my favorite channel—National Geographic. As we wound down for the night, my spirits were ready to really come alive. After helping out with the dishes and other chores around the house, I boldly ventured where no man had gone before: Yes, yes, the "come hither" look said it all. The day was ending but the night had just begun.

I needed a shower, to wash the days activities off me, and to freshen up as well. The boys were tucked into bed, and the bedroom was our next stop. Thus ensued remarkable chemistry that lead to a chain of physiologic responses in my body, which I was shortly going to learn much about. The ying and yang were balanced. Yet such are the powers that be, that we ordinary mortals cannot understand the capriciousness of it all. As the evening progressed, with the boys asleep, our metabolic activity shot way up, and I looked forward to sleeping well tonight while holding my sweetie in my arms tightly.

Everything was perfect. There was light perspiration on my torso as I commented to Doreen that she had the skills of an entire harem all in one body. Alas I may have jinxed myself in my ecstasy for it could not have been more than a few moments later that I noticed my chest started tingling, even the hair roots in my skin ached. Yes, my wife was extraordinary to-night. The sensation became more intense very rapidly, spreading across my whole torso. My nipples became extraordinarily sensitive, almost becoming uncomfortable and shortly later unbearable. The tingling became more severe, almost burning, and spread to the base of my neck. I had a catch in my back muscles and then a slight pressure enveloped me, like a scarf that was wrapped around me. Light as that was it was a harbinger of worse pains to follow. There was no need for alarm yet, this could be just a normal body reaction to intense activity. Not much more time elapsed and the scarf became a vice, squeezing my chest from all around and an inordinate pressure build up on my sternum . Concerned now thinking I had sprained some ligaments severely I reluctantly asked for a time out. This needed to be sorted out; it was deflating the moment and my ego. No thoughts entered my head except that I was going through a temporary muscle cramp or something of the sort. On a pain scale of one through ten it was a modest two, but its presentation was awkward. I stretched my torso trying to undo the knot[s] only to feel it step up a notch, there was definitely something amiss on this occasion, the night had lost its thrill, but yet no need for alarm bells to go off. The pressure encircled my chest broadly front to back, side to side, ran down my left arm to my elbow. My biceps ached as if I had held a heavy box for too long, and now, strangely, my lower jaw and teeth began to ache—lightly at first but building rapidly.

All feelings of ecstasy were evaporating, this was definitely uncomfortable and the first inklings of doubt crept into my mind; apprehension took over, and then even stronger feelings of self-preservation began to emerge. My tentative diagnosis was angina or worse a heart attack. Clinically the diagnosis was straight forward and its progression text book perfect. it starts with light chest discomfort after a certain amount of activity. Quickly it becomes a band or vice around the chest. It may spread to the neck, arms and lower jaw where it may mimics a tooth abscess. I've had a few patients who had stayed awake the whole night in discomfort waiting for me at my office in the morning only to be rushed to the ER in minutes to rule out a cardiac event. I was more often right than wrong. The ones that were not an MI [myocardial infarction or in lay persons terms a heart attack] turned out to be a dissecting AAA [abdominal aortic aneurysm]or another similar related medical emergency.

I kept a doctor's first aid kit at home. Stocked with the usual supplies, I could cope with the usual household emergencies for family and friends such as urinary infections, a yeast infection, cuts and lacerations, migraines, etc. Fortunately, a bottle of nitro was included. Doreen looked puzzled as I asked her to get me that bottle. Mostly I had kept my concerns to myself yet had asked for a time out. Now I spoke up not sure that I believed myself. All thoughts of pleasure were gone; The Don

Juan in me had evaporated. Doreen thought I was playing a prank and a strange one at that. But I didn't look as if it was a joke. When she returned her look told me that what I was suspecting might be true, although she did not know what I was thinking and even I had to fight severe feelings of denial. The discomfort heightened even as the nitro eased me, that is there were different components to the symptoms of discomfort, some eased up while others kept up their intensity, but overall the discomfort was mounting. Perhaps it was a soft three. Beads of sweat and worry moistened my body. My wife's furrowed expression mirrored my discomfort.

"Tell me you are joking," she begged. "Please stop, I'm getting nervous."

She was puzzled, thinking, I could be a clown sometimes but this was out of character for me. Surrealism permeated me: it could not be happening, I was on forty-eight years of age and on top of my game. Things were always tough, but I thrived on challenges, heaping them up on myself layer by layer, invincible, to myself. I was as close to being rock solid as I ever was, and so I was not given to thoughts of premature heart disease. As the vice tightened the proverbial elephant's foot descended upon me. Very real I could trace its footprint on my chest. Fright is a very powerful motivator for good or bad. Two young boys were waiting to see their father in the morning. At this moment I recalled the days when intimacy was an issue because the lads in their younger days always slept with their mom and then me as they grew up. They seemed so young and fragile as the inevitable subjugated my mind. I willed my pain to dissipate only to realize I was mortal. Please could we stop this charade right now and replay this whole evening? Really, I could do without this right now; there were more pressing issues to attend to shortly, real life events not this crap.

I pushed aside my strongest virtue—bullheadedness—and told Doreen to call 911. The pain had become very distinct, it had flooded me, there was no escaping it, I could ignore it and die a horrible death tonight or give myself the benefit of a doubt and do the right thing. There had been too many instances of couples falling asleep, only for the wife to wake up in the morning besides her husband's cold dead body. From unapologetic nirvana to near apoplexy in a short duration, that was a macabre thought but powerful enough to motivate me. She made me repeat myself and falteringly I did so. Tears welled up.

"What is happening?"

"I think I'm having a heart attack," I mumbled.

She still had not accepted my words, and I would have done the same if I were in her shoes. Things had progressed that fast, perhaps ten minutes into the ordeal.

I listened to the call being made, it seemed strange that I was the patient and this was my first ambulance ride. What would the neighbors think?

It was then that my eldest awoke and dashed into the room. I was too afraid to reassure him, the poor boy. I wanted to reach for him but could not move. To this day I feel that I did not touch or reach out to him before I left the house. His face showed much anguish, he was much too young to be witnessing his father going to the hospital. If I could have left him with one thought it would have been, "take care of mum and your brother while I am gone".

Within five minutes of the call, firemen arrived and shortly thereafter an ambulance. After a cursory exam, the EMT reported he had a patient going to the ER with a flu that was causing chest discomfort. He checked my vital signs, placed leads on my chest, and started an I.V. I was bundled up in blankets and deposited on a transport gurney. The short ride from the bedroom through the living room and bumping over the threshold into the cool air revived me some. I preferred keeping my eyes closed. The ambulance could not have gone fast enough. Although the lights were flashing, the siren was not on. We rolled toward the hospital at a sedate pace.

Could they not pick it up? I was at a steady level four or five on the pain scale. The lack of concern gave me great concern. The lack of sirens and the sedate pace indicated I was not being taken seriously. The EMT's brushed my concerns aside, they had seen it too often, callused came to mind. Some mumblings ensued, but no change in pace. A vague Globus [difficulty swallowing] feeling settled in my throat, no doubt secondary to feelings of anxiety and the helplessness I was feeling. As we finally pulled into the ambulance bay outside the E.R. some of the tension subsided, there were caring individuals beyond the double doors who would take over. When I rolled into the E.R., all pride and formality was set aside by my discomfort, I needed relief and quickly, that was paramount to me, the discomfort ratcheting another half notch again. Friendly faces looked at me but seemed not to recognize my countenance, perhaps my features were scrunched up too much. I was completely out of context. The staff might have realized that a doctor as belligerent as I was reputed to be was arriving in an ambulance would need aid quickly. Never in my career had I ever heard of a doctor taking an ambulance to a E.R. It should have set off warning bells. No such luck, today.

MY ER STAY

What is angina? It is simply described as chest pain caused by lack of blood to certain parts of the heart. This is caused by obstruction of a blood vessel or spasms of the same. It may also be referred to as chest pain. Looking into the blood vessels of the heart may reveal atherosclerosis [cholesterol and other blood cells] buildup against the side of the blood vessels and blood clots obstructing the lumen. It becomes even more complicated with anginal equivalents, i.e. pain sensations referred to other body parts. My discomfort started predictably developing upon severe exertion, starting slow and low, building up predictably as the blood vessel [in the heart] got sealed off. As more heart muscle gets asphyxiated the discomfort spreads to the entire chest, from the belly button to the jaw. Radiation or spreading occurs to the shoulders, back, arms and neck [occasionally these pieces of referred discomfort may be the only sign of impending heart disease], confounding the clinician. Non heart causes of angina may include sprained chest wall, stomach ulcers, gall bladder disease, acid reflux, stress, generalized anxiety, pulmonary embolism [blood clot in the lungs], dissecting [tearing] aneurysm, pleurisy and about a hundred more causes .Diagnosis is based on the history of the patient, his medical back ground, risk factors, age at presentation, prior medical events and a skill honed sharp by many years of practice. Certain blood tests and the electrical activity [heart monitor] help with the diagnosis .What else may be happening during a E.R. visit. The physician has to attend to other patients presenting continuously to this department, all with various levels of sickness, there may be constant interruptions, the need to review labs, rays and other tests. Other physicians will be calling in to inquire of their patients, specialists have to be called in to consult on other patients, throw in an occasional emergency on the floors upstairs which the E.R. staff may have to respond to, throw in paperwork, distraught family members demanding answers and you get a piece of the picture. This is for a Level One or Two medical centers. Advance to a level Three and magnify everything by a factor of Three. Thus it is challenging to be a patient or staff in this situation even more for the latter who do it on a daily basis. Think Compassion Burnout.

Even as the nurse took a report from the ambulance crew, all agreed that I was having flu-like symptoms. I was triaged to the non-emergent or the ambulatory side of the ER. This is where patients deemed not as sick are put in sick bays for a more relaxed visit after the critical ones have been seen or a more junior staff is assigned to care for them. As my vital signs were checked a second IV started, a medical professional started to examine me and seemed confused at the ashen look of my features. My description of discomfort was out of proportion to the report he had received. I saw his confusion even as I felt a loss of autonomy and independence. Clearly he did not know what to do. There were conflicting stories and which one was he to believe, a simple flu or angina possibly leading to a heart attack. I could be a malingerer or displaying drug seeking behavior. I became just another patient going through the system. The staff went along with the paramedics' initial diagnosis of flu-like symptoms, and I started to stress that I was having severe chest discomfort. But this only led to cross-questioning of myself. I felt the tide turning against me viciously and pictured myself with a possible lethal condition, trying to convince some idiotic know-it-all that I knew what was wrong with me. How many times had he heard this before [a lot]; how many times had he heard it from a senior staff physician coming in by ambulance, presumably this was his first time and hopefully his last. In retrospect this medical provider would remember me for a long time to come.

Where was my wife? I felt so abandoned. In this same ER where I worked often enough for many staff to know me by my first name, no one seemed to recognize me or out of professionalism chose to ignore their relationship with me.

I was pacified told I would be okay and taken care of. The pace was sedate, no one seemed too impressed. Staff exchanged looks among themselves—another hypochondriac exaggerating his symptoms. Let him be.

Soon the room cleared, and the lump in my throat got painful. Is this what an innocent man felt just before his lethal injection? Though I did not feel like I was dead, I had a horrendous feeling of being abandoned, and no one was in my corner. My small room was sterile; my caretakers more like jail wardens, compassion had been beaten out of us a long time ago although we always wanted to be seen as considerate. But things would get worse, much worse before I would get the right treatment. Between now and then several eternities would pass before the night was through for me.

And then my angel appeared. A nurse having finished her twelve hour shift was walking out passed by the board recognized my name on the patient list at the desk and came to see who it was. Immediately she recognized me and saw the discomfort I was in. She asked what was wrong. I made a quick summary and assessment of my symptoms.

"Don't you worry, Dr. Castellino," she said. She summoned my nurse and told her, "This is Dr. Castellino. He looks really bad. The doctor should see him right away, and he should be on the acute side". Finally, a sense of relief flooded me. My care should now be prompt and decisive, after all someone had spoken up for me and her assessment was spot on. My karma had to change going forward, yes, yes ,yes.

The nurse summoned my provider, and he got the same message: "You guys are making a mistake. He looks very sick and should be in the ICU room [where they keep the most critical patients]. The doctor should see him right away"

The mid-level looked confused. He was relying on the paramedic's diagnosis of chest flu. Yet I looked quite ill, and now a nurse was telling him that this was a practicing physician in the community who was possibly having a heart attack, and he should be moved to the acute side. Reluctantly, he proceeded to follow her directions, probably relieved though to be free of a case that seemed to be rapidly evolving into something complicated. I was moved to the critical care room. Finally someone was going to do the right thing. Was it going to be enough though?

I was hooked up to a heart monitor. Hearing the steady beeps assured me that at least my heart rhythm was normal. But where was the physician who was to look at me. The general staff seemed unimpressed by my condition, and I actually felt ignored. A lackadaisical attitude, and yet the chest discomfort kept growing. I knew what was happening; I was a physician. Couldn't they see that? I tried to impress on the staff what I felt was wrong, and yet I only got a look of annoyance: "Leave us alone. We know how to take care of you."

Doreen had finally arrived. She had gotten lost in finding parking and then navigating her way to the Emergency Department. Gripping my sweaty palm there was reassurance that someone was there for me. The minutes ticked by, yet not much time had elapsed. The steel rails of the gurney felt cold and refreshing against my moist sticky skin. The gown around me frequently came undone. My wife, always mindful of decorum, kept adjusting it as I grimaced. Much later she related that by looking at my countenance she felt my suffering yet felt helpless to ease my pain and discomfort.

My will to live and be my own advocate was sorely tested by my discomfort. There was a real fear here that I would not even be around when the doctor would come. My judgment was impaired by several factors: pain, fatigue, apprehension. I was already looking at my soon-to-be widowed wife and thinking of my two fatherless sons, as if my fears had already become reality. Prompted by this impending disaster, I focused myself, asked Doreen to go to the desk and summon a physician. She returned to say that someone would be in soon.

Yes, but when?

If this had been a restaurant by now I would have asked to speak to the Maître; if this was a hotel room I would have been on the line with the front desk, yet who to contact now to press my case forwards. Have we as a medical community seen so much suffering that we have become immune to its presentation, have we forgotten why we joined the profession in the first place.

Soon enough thereafter a physician arrived. Normally an interview with a physician follows a definite pattern: description of symptoms, duration, severity, location, radiation, previous history, and so on. Yet this dialogue lasted but a minute or so. The hospital bill we later received documented a full visit and a comprehensive examination.

"Don't worry. We'll take care of you. Relax, rest. We'll do some tests and figure out what's happening."

And she was gone.

"That was it?" I thought to myself! Wasn't there even the courtesy of recognizing that a colleague was in your ER and under your care? Had we all become so desensitized that we didn't even care about the person and the personality that distinguishes us from each other? I was not asking for special treatment, just what was customary and usual for a patient in my condition. I wanted to be listened to and taken more seriously. I would have liked some pain relief The fact that I had been on staff for fifteen years at this very hospital should have made my care a little more personable, more humane.

This was brutal, insensitive care at its worse. I felt I was taking up her time. She really didn't want to be bothered with caring for me. At least recognizing a fellow colleague would have been reassuring. I looked at my wife to see if she concurred. But mirrored in her expression was the pain I was feeling; she had not paid attention to the conversation.

Shortly the various ER technicians came in, one to do an EKG (this measures the electrical activity of the heart and may help to make the diagnosis of various diseases, including heart attacks). Another came to do lab tests, including a test I assumed was a CPK and a troponin level. These are chemicals found in the blood during a heart attack; their levels vary with the time of presentation, severity and other factors, but all these are taken into account in the emergency room and other settings. Together with an EKG, these tests can provide a comprehensive picture of what is happening to a heart in an emergent situation.

Even as I waited, my pain discomfort level escalated, pulled back slightly, and then went up again. There was a very slow but steady increase in discomfiture.

Not being able to take much more, I asked for some pain relief medication. I was asked to wait till the test levels were back. Agonizingly I writhed on the ER gurney; my wife's presence soothed me although I did not look much in her direction. She told me later she paced the room, but I thought she was sitting behind my left shoulder all the while. I repeated my request for some type of pain relief again. I described my pain level as a greater than 10, which is supposedly not possible, yet that is what I felt. Eventually I recalled that I maxxed out my pain level at fourteen over ten, at that level you will sell your soul to the devil or your family into slavery for an aliquot of pain relief. Nothing else comes to mind except relief, that blocks out everything else. And yet everybody and everything moved in slow motion unconcerned about my predicament.

My request was relayed to the physician and yet no relief. Normally I am a person of action, and the perceived lack of it frightened me. I thought of what I could do to help myself and came up bereft. My friends were physicians and some of them were probably up on the floors doing their rounds but they would have come to my assistance if beckoned and willingly so. However there was a possibility that this episode was nothing and I would be bothering them for naught, and so I counted time. If only I had listened to my intuition some more, the outcome might have been less severe, damn me. I tried to play mind games with myself, and yet that didn't work. The waves of pain swept over me emanating in and around my chest. I recollect that they were waves but with many ripples, however never did it drop to a comfortable level. I described the level as twelve out of ten and heading upwards. Again I requested some intervention for my pain relief, using my wife as an interloper who would seek a person who would relay my message to the nurse or doctor. No relief came, however my physician did enter the room and told me my studies were negative! Before I could discuss what were we to do next she had left! This was becoming my Auschitwz.

There was no evidence of a heart attack that they could discern on the tests. But the pain was real, crushing, incapacitating, frightening, and persistent. Was it all a figment of my imagination? Was I making it all up so well that I was confusing myself? Perhaps I was at fault; I always had an overactive imagination. Could I have hallucinated this all up and fooled myself?

I was paralyzed with my thoughts, pain, and the lack of evidence that was reported to me. I needed relief from the pain.

A couple of years later I had a chance to speak with the E.R. Director about my stay at his department. I had waited that long to let issues cool off a bit and sanity to prevail. He actually denied knowing that I had passed through his department as a patient and proceeded to bully me into keeping quiet. Retrospectively I should have acted sooner; alas hindsight is always too late.

Sometime later Doreen described me as an earthworm wriggling on the gurney trying to burrow itself but with nowhere to go. I tried to connect the dots to make sense. There had to be a logical explanation. I tried to be my advocate and yet presented with the evidence to date, I befuddled myself even more, which was not very difficult to do. However the discomfort had to be addressed, once again I communicated to the staff the need for pain management. Finally I was told something was coming. My wife told me I received something in my IV. Yes, yes there was going to be relief.

In a few moments there was a slow decline in my pain level and surely things were going to get better. But the respite was only transient; waves of discomfort resumed their ferocity even more severely. This was really exhausting in its savagery, I wanted to throw in the towel and quit, but how does one quit on life, on living. There was no plug to be pulled. I had to muddle through with the game to its very end. But what was the game? What were the rules? How was it played? When was one a victor or vanquished?

There was so much pain that it confused my senses. My will for self-preservation would not let me quit. Actually, it was the need to seek relief from the pain that ruled me. What do I do next? No one else seemed interested in my predicament. My wife stood beside me, but she was not versed in critical and emergent care medicine and didn't know how to help me. It must have been rough upon her to watch me and be unable to help.

On several occasions I summoned help. Something needed to be done to get a diagnosis. I remained in a state of agitated prostration, still grasping for straws to help myself. How far could this go on? How much more could I take? I tried to reassure myself once again that things would be all right, but the agonizing waves of pain left my body gasping for breath. Everything would be okay if I could just hold on for a while more.

Through my wife I asked for some additional relief from the pain, I believe several times I received doses of morphine in small aliquots, I learned afterward totaling 18 milligrams, Total. Yet there was barely a touch of relief. I didn't even know when the boluses were given, yet my wife said I was somewhat out of it, and medical personnel did administer them to me periodically. Once again I asked to speak to my physician, who did return. She continued to reassure me that once the CT of my chest was done we would know what was wrong. What was the physician thinking when she ordered the C.T. some discourse with me would have helped.

But why the holdup, shouldn't I have been scanned by now. Maybe the machine was down; maybe the on call x-ray tech was on his way in. I again asked for a repeat of my heart enzymes and an EKG, this is standard practice in a person with chest pain of unknown cause which was denied. It was a simple request, but this wasn't my lucky day.

Giving up the pretense of a stoic any more, having had enough I asked my wife to summon my acquaintance a cardiologist, who also happened to be a good family and personal friend. Our wives and children had often been together at many celebrations. He would make things right. Doreen left my side to go to the front desk and ask that he be paged. I rested briefly as I saw her return, reassuring me the call had been made. I awaited some change in my care, yet time stood still and trickled on. Finally I received word the he was on his way in and had ordered the tests to be done that I had asked for.

Medical personnel returned to my room and placed leads from the EKG machine on my chest to display the electrical activity of my heart. The recording was briefly put on hold while a lab technician put a tourniquet on my arm and drew a fresh blood sample. I didn't feel the prick of the needle; it was minor compared to what else I felt. The EKG tech was again by my side. I heard the stylus rub against the paper being pushed out by the machine.

"Please be still," I was told. My movements had interfered with the recording that would have to be redone. I tried to lie still, trying to help myself and finally an EKG reading was obtained.

"Holy crap!" the tech uttered. "This guy is having an acute MI (that is, a heart attack).

I lapsed into a more restful state right away. I was vindicated but could not celebrate my victory. There was change in my care immediately. The cadence of speech had changed around me, it had become terse, some apprehension had finally built up around me and that indicated I was a priority now. Somebody always seemed to be hovering around me showing consideration and gasp, even emotion. Even my doctor returned shortly inquired about my pain status. I was given more meds, which seemed to sedate me yet did little for the pain. Word came in from the lab that my enzymes tested positive for a heart attack.

I heard a discussion around me that I could not fully comprehend and then there was a big step up in my level of care. It was palpable. There was a sense of energy and purpose.

The enemy was known and thus the objective was clear. I did know not what medications I was given, but it would include, aspirin, a beta blocker that would slow the heart rate down, TPA to dissolve clots in the body, nitroglycerine to dilate my heart blood vessels thus bringing more blood to my obstruction and relieving my discomfort. All these medications along with others were designed for one thing, to promptly relieve the obstruction and save my heart muscle, relieving me of a lot of potential complications like an irregular heart rate, congestive heart failure chronic angina or chest pain, fluid buildup in the lungs and others. Relief would be prompt once the meds were administered. Staff asked me to straighten my arms so more IVs could be placed. Even as I looked at the nurse, my son stood at the doorway of my room looking at me with concern yet oddly separated from the events unfolding. I summoned him with my outstretched hand; he looked at me yet did not come closer. I summoned him again, yet no response. My nurse was short with me to lay my arm straight. I told him I was calling my son who was behind him.

There is no one there he told me. I asked Doreen to call him again and she asked, "Who?"

"Wayne," I said.

She replied that he was not there but had stayed at home to be with his younger brother.

"What? I see him right there."

But he was not there anymore. I refused to believe my wife or the nurse, but Wayne did not respond when I faintly called. After my hospitalization I had asked him about seeing him in the E.R., his reply was that he had stayed at home to be with the youngest and yes I had imagined him there, but why.

Someone else appeared, though: my cardiologist. He spoke briefly to me and my wife, paying attention to the monitor above me. I needed to be moved to a hospital specializing in heart patients and fast. Someone was finally in my corner and I could relax. The staff seemed so attentive now, which felt good after being treated as a problem patient. I heard glimpses of conversation of various staff members sometimes with my wife. A helicopter was mentioned, but the chopper was not available, bad weather or motor problems. Concise and precise orders flowed fast. People knew that they had a fight on their hands guided by my cardiologist,[he was respected, thus his word carried authority and guidance]. Doctors were called at the other hospital, alerted of my critical status, that I would need an emergent catheterization of my heart. I heard my blood pressure was low and falling.

Even as relief flooded my body, the pain balanced any feelings of immediate salvation. But I was elated. I was right, and I was going to be saved.

My vision started to get blurry. It took me a few moments to focus. My tongue felt thick and heavy; my limbs held down by invisible restraints. Someone told my wife that I was going on another ambulance ride to a hospital in another town, where they'd give me a higher level of care. She looked at me, and I nodded that this was okay.

Another ambulance crew quickly arrived, and I was prepared for my next journey. There was no wasted time or actions. Were it not for the pain I would have been smiling. I held my wife's hand as I was cautiously wheeled to the ambulance bay. My cardiologist was nearby, a frown crinkled his forehead, and his gaze seemed too focused for my comfort.

I would not let go of Doreen's hand. Repeatedly I murmured, "I'm sorry, I'm sorry, I'm sorry."

"Why?" she asked.

I just repeated myself. "I'm sorry, I'm sorry, I'm sorry." Much later, she asked me why I said those words. I still have not told her, but I knew all along. I knew the journey had just begun and that it was going to be long tumultuous ride. The look of concern on my cardiologist's face, the ongoing chest pressure in spite of all necessary meds, my falling blood pressure, and the blurry vision told me that a near calamity was to follow. I knew my wife was going to experience a harrowing life-changing event. I wished I could turn the doctor part of my brain off; I know that would help me relax more. But yet my instinct for self-preservation would not let me put my guard down.

In a situation such as mine the next thing to do is to put a catheter into the heart from the groin. The purpose of the catheter is to take pictures of the blood vessels in the heart, identify the site of blockage, administer medications, and place a device called a stent. This is a collapsed hollow tube that is placed over the site of the blockage. It can be opened after being placed in a location and then expanded, squishing the blockage against the side of the blood vessels and opening up the blood flow. This decreases the discomfort; saving valuable heart tissue and helping the individual regain heart function as close to normal as possible. The procedure is fraught with complications, but performed by a skilled operator it is fairly routine.

So who gets open-heart surgery? Those patients with several blood vessels affected, those with compromised heart function, and when the blockage is in a location where placing a stent is not feasible or too risky. All this information is obtained during the heart catheterization, while pictures are being taken and other functions are checked.

If any complications occur during the procedure, it would be stopped and the open-heart team would be called in to for surgery. What was going to be my outcome? I would know soon enough, but it was an answer that I only somewhat wanted to know. It was part of the game you could not quit and had to be played till the end.

This reminded me of an ancient Aztec game, ullamaliztli. In this game two warriors faced off and knocked a ball about twelve feet into the air with their hips. The opponent passed it back similarly. The loser was ritually sacrificed. Though it was considered a honor to ends one's life this way, I felt like nothing like a warrior, in fact, quite the opposite.

I was bundled in blankets and moved onto a gurney and placed into the ambulance. My wife held my hand as they rolled me toward the ambulance bay. A crack in the door let the cool evening air against my face, pleasantly distracting me for a moment from my predicament. My discomfort momentarily eased as the pleasant sensation continued. We will grab onto anything to save us from a painful fate, even for a fleeting period.

Once again the waves of pain returned and then abated. My anxiety also returned. I sensed a fresh IV being placed on my other arm. I requested and received another bolus of pain meds. Narcosis was clouding my judgment and distorting reality. I held on one-half confused the other totally disoriented, and yet the discomfort pierced the cloud to reach my consciousness. I felt more off than on with brief periods of respite. My last few thoughts were with Doreen. Would she stay where we lived or would she choose to live near her sisters? Where would the boys go to school? Would either of them choose to be physicians, and how would this experience change them for the future? Were they too young to remember much? Why was all this important now? Befuddled I wanted to lapse into unconsciousness. My mind was heavy, sounds were distorted, and slight nausea rolled over me. Closing my eyes I prayed for the ordeal to end. I asked God what he wanted of me, but no voice answered.

But I heard other voices.

"Jesus, his BP is 60 over palp (a very low blood pressure at which you pass it out). Can we go any faster?"

"I'm already doing 90, can you give him another bolus of IV fluids?" the driver boomed back.

"Radio the hospital. He's going to need help right at the door." The faint voices trailed into an echo. There were fainter replies from the handset and several commands. I don't really know if my recollection was absolutely right, these are the exact thoughts that still float through my head over these last few years. But it does not consume me like it used to.

THE AMBULANCE RIDE

With numerous infusions going, probably the medications that had been started in the last half hour I was swaddled in blankets and rushed to a waiting ambulance. Back through the bay doors I went. The cool wind found every crack in the coverings and tickled my insides giving me a chance to enjoy a counter sensation on myself, to distract myself again. One EMT pushed and the other pulled, they were anxious to get a move on. No motion or time was dwelled on. I kept on thinking the meds would kick in soon and relief was imminent, [alas too much heart muscle was compromised and too far gone for rescue, thus there would be suffering for some time to come], yet I was deluding myself, holding onto straws . Jerking as we took off, the lights spun taking an unearthly jaundiced color, making my gastric contents bounce around. The gentle rocking motion of the ambulance as it pulled out, sirens off lulled me. Ahh; the small things in life that make a difference. Befuddled as I was, it was difficult to know if I was having nonsensical thoughts brought on by meds probably Morphine or my level of cognizance was diminishing, as supported by my low blood pressure; Probably both. Why were the sirens not on yet, came to mind, I could not take another snail ride, but there was temperance knowing I was heading to a location where definitive treatment would be available.

"This guy looks bad," I heard, as my two techs made me ready for the ride and the receiving facility. Their situation was precarious; it is not good form to leave one facility with a live cargo and to present a corpse at the other. Not on their shift. Intent, they spoke as needed only, carefully stewarding their precious cargo. Anything that distracted me seemed to give relief, no matter how small. I studied whatever was around me, the equipment; most of it was to resuscitate patients. The rig slowly rolled toward the freeway, about two hundred yards away, I saw the turn on approaching. Suddenly it came alive: tires screeched several whoops on the horn, sirens came on, lights flashed, my head knocked some railings unable to control itself. Speed picked up rapidly as I slid around but I willed myself to go even faster. Not that my life depended on it (I'm a crappy patient). As I slipped in and out of a trance-like state, more info was discussed about me, perhaps they thought I was not there mentally, and that was fine too just put metal to the pedal.

It felt like a minute later when he said, "His BP is 64 over palp, O2 sat is 92, skin cold and clammy."[these are the vital signs of a person near imminent collapse] Hearing his words, knowing the pain was escalating, thoughts were befuddled, and judgment impaired, I was going to pass out soon, but not before I held my missus again .I didn't want to go out like this with no last good bye. That was for soldiers on far flung battle fields. Where was Wayne, I'm sure I had seen him, yet why did the wife say he was not there, a conspiracy was on.

The vital signs that were relayed to the receiving hospital were numbers that did not inspire confidence. They asked if I was comatose or not. Cardiogenic shock was mentioned, other indistinguishable were cited. Had their voice dropped down a pitch or two, words ran into each other, not that it mattered much, I was beyond caring. The pain had not sub-sided, indicating that more damage was occurring, and I would only get sicker.

I dearly believed in God at that moment. I was sick and the pain was murderous. The narcotics did a good job of snowing me, but inwardly I said, "God, it is okay to take me away from this suffering. Please forgive me my sins. Take care of my family, the wife and young boys ,they are blameless and deserve better "And I negotiated for peace terms.

"What can I do right now to relieve me of this distress, speak tell me what, you can't really be doing this to me, I'm special, let's talk this through".

But no one spoke to me. I thought a miracle was due at any minute, as if I might be that someone special and divine intervention was my prerogative.

One of the medics asked, "Is he one of the local docs? His name sounds familiar. Can we make this rig go any faster!" he asked.

"I'm doing ninety, dude," the driver replied.

"Radio the hospital; he is going to need assistance at the door to make it".

The usual sixty-minute ambulance ride was done in forty, but it seemed to me like they were moving in slow motion. My surroundings started to turn gray. Voices became distant. My wife; was-where? I was frightened not for myself but my unaccomplished mission. I had been wrapped in the American immigrant's dream of hard work and sacrifice that would make everything would fall in place. But now I thought of all the wasted years on foolishness. I thought of the void within and without. Things I had not said, time with the boys I had not taken, the damage I had done to my psyche, and the foolishness of thinking about it now. I had sacrificed everything: my wife, my family, and myself. Perhaps this was my folly and my sentence, meted out together. Now I was going to leave without leaving a mark on this earth; or rather I was going to be remembered for foolishness rather than any outstanding achievements.

I sensed when we left the freeway again, now in the next city and threaded through the city streets toward the hospital. The rocking felt comfortable. Though not much consciousness was left, dimly I perceived the streetlights hitting me again me on the face as we continued. The rig stayed dimly lit. Or was it my faint vision? There was not much of me in the conscious world now, only snippets of chatter, fragments of thoughts drifted through me. Objects seemed to float, my pain receded, and speech was incoherent when there was any. Our rig had stopped, abruptly, tires screeching, loose objects rolling and swinging, yes the urgency or panic was impending.

Again I felt more blankets being tucked under and over me. I heard snippets of conversation, but I can't recall much of their context. New voices were heard, none known to me. The tone was somber, rushed and precise. I was unhooked and re hooked to hospital equipment at a frightening speed, these guys were on the ball.

Feeling a bump we crossed into the other hospital at a run. The receiving nurse said they were calling for me to the catheterization lab stat. [this is a mini surgical room where they pass certain devices into the heart to interrogate it and determine what needs to be done next. Could they fix it or would open heart surgery be next]. I never did find out until several days later. A doctor had come there before me and was anxious to start the procedure on me. No doubt my friend Mani from back home had called and impressed upon them my situation not that anyone needed to know the obvious. My presentation and development was textbook perfect. Later I realized it was about one thirty in the morning. Just about then my lights went out mercifully, slipping into the land of Hades.

When I awoke, my wife was looking down at me with moisture in her eyes. She seemed tired, but cautiously relieved. There was sunlight streaming in my room slightly dusky, yet refreshing. I heard birds chirping but could not see them. Doreen looked like she wanted to speak, but she held back. She had aged overnight.

I felt tremendously relaxed, refreshed, and buoyant. The night had gone well it seemed, my fears had been unfounded. I was awake, pain free.

'Pain free!' yes, yes, yes. This was high reward indeed. My muscles were sore, but the discomfort was relieved, maybe what happened last night was in fact an aberration, or the procedure was a total success. Rubbing my chest it was flat, no scars or bruises. There was no midline scar, no zipper [colloquial description for open heart surgery] for all this had happened overnight! I had over exaggerated after all, otherwise how could I explain this miraculous overnight recovery. Stretching there were some discomfort but otherwise I was elated, the doctor and team had done a bang up job. But why was Doreen crying and trembling?

Ah, women are always sentimental. We men are strong and not one to give in to the vagaries of our emotion. Good , enough of all this hullaballoo, I should be back to work in a day or so, I had badly reacted to last night's events.

2

THE AWAKENING

My wife studied me as if I did not perceive her presence. What was she looking at? I surmised she was not familiar with medical mumbo jumbo, monitors, continuous EKG readings, etc. Little did I know how far she had come? It was I, my pompous self who was in the dark. Presently it dawned on me she was looking to see if there was any cerebral activity besides the open eyes was there signs of recognition, was I tracking her movements, was my look blank or with recognition [these simple features would be the early harbinger of brain damage or stability]

Sternly she asked me my name.

"Why?" I asked.

"Just answer."

"Conrad," I said.

"Where are you?"

"Well, at the other hospital."

"Who am I?"

"My wife, Doreen."

I sensed her relief with each answer.

"Why are you asking me this?"

"Just answer me."

"Okay, I'll play along."

"Why did you come here?"

"I had a heart attack last night."

There was sudden pupil dilation, her posture stiffened, almost withdrawing from me I was confused but still elated things had gone along so well.

"When did you come here?"

"Last night, Doreen, but. . ."

"Be quiet. What day is it?"

"Well you brought me here last night, which was Tuesday, so now it is Wednesday." Hah I was right, I knew everything, and cockiness crept back in my voice.

There was a firm squeeze of my hand while her hand rested on my chest, which had been shaved, though not by an esthetician I guessed. Now it was her turn to be silent. She seemed relieved and exhausted, but tears rolled off her cheeks and onto my bed sheet. Could this drama stop now, I was alright, when would I be going home!.

I stared. Something was wrong. I looked for clues. I was hooked to a lot of equipment. I felt jubilant, so what gives?

The monitors beeped my steady rhythm but seemed to hiccup some. There was a whooshing repetitious sound. An empty IV bag swayed from the pole. I felt rather large painful swellings in my groin, no doubt where they had gone in to the aorta, a big blood vessel in the center of the body. There were multiple IV marks on my extremities and a huge crater on the roof of my mouth. My limbs felt heavy yet looked skinny.

"Conrad, I brought you here last week on Tuesday. Now it is Thursday of the next week!" she weakly replied.

Was she joking? We looked at each other in silence. I surveyed my surroundings. There were so many IVs, so many pieces of medical equipment. Could I be or had I been that sick?

"Something bad happened to me?"

"Yes". Her voice seemed stronger.

I felt her words were true, however it was not time for me to know, there was a possibility I was still dreaming. However the scars on my body, the skin punctures, groin swellings told me much. I had seen similar evidence on others, and so putting the evidence together a story was emerging. My professional training said a catastrophe had occurred.

"Was I very sick?". She nodded in the affirmative. Infinity raced by in a few blinks of an eye. My disposition was being shredded. It was not difficult to put the story together. The implications of what I was just told were staggering, and although not knowing the details I could start to surmise the rest.

I could not care right then any more, exhausted, I needed to rest, go to sleep. My eyes closed in fatigue.

Later that day there were many well-wishers in the room, too many, word had gotten out I was awake. It had started the next evening [after I had been admitted into the hospital] after offices had closed. Today, I was tired again but elated, trying to speak my thick tongue made out nonsensical syllables. Eyes Dilated wide studying me. Did he have a stroke too. They were all staring at me; it became obvious when I thought of it later. I was on display a macabre phenomenon, they were gawking, taking mental bets, was I there mentally, was my brain toasted, would I make it. It was more that they spoke around me than at me. The news and their impressions had to be broadcasted as soon possible. This was all deciphered many years later when reliving my experiences. I was weak and could barely put a glass to my mouth. Doreen told me there was a stream of visitors starting the next evening after I was admitted, when news had gotten out and offices had started to close, and with members of my family in attendance the waiting room was full. My mother seemed to take it harder than the rest and was passionate. As my liver suffered under the metabolic burden it started to malfunction, liver enzymes went up somewhat similar to an alcoholic liver[indicating severe problems in that organ].

Thus my family was asked if I was an alcoholic by a well-meaning nurse. This was explained the next day to be a condition known as 'Toxic shock liver' or 'Hypoxic Encephalopathy', but the damage was done. To this day I am still considered an alcoholic because of a ill placed conversation with the wrong people. I have also in the same vein am supposed to have had a a stroke as I stuttered and uttered gibberish initially as my synapses took time to reestablish channels of thought and fluency in my initial conversation.

One of my visitors, a doctor friend, was heard talking in the waiting room that I would not make it. It was an off the cuff remark or displaying his prowess. He did not know my brothers and sister were in the room listening in. There was much consternation—and panic. However when they rushed in I was unchanged, yet comatose.

The next day even more visitors streamed in. I had a high fever, so I was placed on a cooling blanket and uncovered a lot, leading Doreen and the nurses in a battle to keep me modest but without a fever. So intense was my condition that I was assigned two nurses to care for me till I got better.

Mercifully that night[the day I woke up] the visitors left, even my wife. She had been with me nonstop for eight days. Now she was back at home with the boys; freshening up, resting, eating meals made by family members, organizing her thoughts. My sister-in-law Colette later told me that one evening she drove Doreen home; immediately she lay down on the couch for a short nap, only to wake up midmorning the next day. Later I learned that all my siblings took turns to be with my wife so that she was never really alone with me. But nevertheless, a seven-day vigil would wear anyone down. They had made sure she ate something and kept her resting on the couch when I was stable. Doreen though never left my side, refusing even to sleep even one night in the hotel across the road, where arrangements had been made to facilitate her into taking some respite.

At times I was restless and my muscles were twitching relentlessly. Then she would speak and I would calm down. Plus mega doses of sedatives were used. Later on, when the twitching's [read seizures] got worse more specific meds were used to calm my oxygen starved brain. As I stayed comatose one evening or morning, a dream came to me that was a very long intense vision and that to this day I think about at least once daily. Thoughts rush back to me, it seemed a blur but my dream plays itself back at me, calming me, soothing me, taking me into its womb, sheltering me from reality. I loved to go there, it was so fresh in my thoughts that I looked around my room for physical evidence of my vision, and I longed to reach out and touch it.

Deep inside I was putting everything together medically, from tidbits I had overheard. But I had not asked for an explanation from friends, family, or staff. There was much else to think about.

The fight for my life was brutal, and there were scars to prove it. What was that huge ulcer on the roof of my mouth? I thought I could rub bone with my swollen tongue. Yet to protect me, my mind had taken me to a distant place. It has been three-plus years since it happened, but I can still recollect every part of it [my dream]. It sustains me, yet it has given me a profound message. I feel I am not worthy of myself to understand and come to terms with who I am and what transpired with me in the most brutal sense before the shroud will be lifted and I understand what message the reverie gave me.

THE DREAM

Not being a particularly a religious man, maybe I should not have been having a dialogue with the man upstairs. However, having no one to hold accountable other than myself, I should have been suffering in solitude. Nevertheless, maybe my upbringing forced me to talk with my creator. I had already gone through my initial three phases of not accepting my fate—denial, conflict and acceptance—the final being resolution.

I thought of my family being left behind and not being able to provide for them, not seeing my boys grow into men and establish themselves. And what would happen to my wife? I thought she would move to where her sisters lived and maybe have to work again. I was already resigned that my life was at an end. Now if only the pain would ease up. I had surrendered. These thoughts raced through my mind in last few minutes on intermittent coherency.

My last conscious memory was being bumped over the hospital threshold and hearing, "They want him up in the cath. lab ASAP."

When I next opened my eyes, Doreen was looking down at me emotional and asking silly questions. Exhausted, I drifted into a slumber hearing what was happening around me, but my mind wandered to what I had been dreaming about.

Between the threshold and the short gurney ride to the heart lab mercifully I was rescued to another plane, dimension, or a place my mind had created to nurse me though my journey. I don't know when my vision started, but it is the only remembrance of the entire time I was in a coma which lasted seven days.

Memories of the dream are as vivid as when I first experienced it. My first recollection was of standing on a dusty path that stretched in a straight line in either direction with no particular distinguishing features other than the sandy bareness that stretched off as far as the eye could see. The road went left and right, straight as an arrow. Here was my first challenge. There was a feeling that I needed to find the right path to go down. Why did I feel this need to go down one direction or the other? Is that not the way in our lives, we always have to make decisions. Doing nothing is not an option, perhaps it should be; But in which direction? And why did I feel this urge to find the right path to follow? I walked toward the right after taking a random guess. As I walked the lifeless path, nothing appealed to me or made me feel that this was a creative decision. Sand dusted my feet and toes.

Yet I kept down the path. Giving up finally as there was no purpose in moving forward, I rested for a while. A drink of water would have done well to cool my parched tongue, but none was to be had. Wind swept up swirls of sand that danced, highlighting the barrenness of the landscape. Feeling foolish at my fruitless labor, I retraced my footsteps back to where I had originally started. Feeling a need to do something that would prove me right, I thus launched into the other direction, not with much conviction though. Again I felt there was going to be no benefit to proceeding further and retraced my path back to the start. Frustrated I sat myself down and pondered my desolate surroundings. Any further ramblings were interrupted by a sudden encounter. A nondescript fellow was sauntering up to me. I was somewhat startled as I had not seen anyone on the path or evidence that any one else had used it. He seemed focused upon me as he approached. He wore loose summer clothing the color of the sandy wastes behind him—sandals, a beach shirt, khaki shorts, but no other adornments.

"Let's go for a swim", he said. There were no greetings or how do you do. Abrupt was his demeanor, yet he changed as events unfolded.

"What? I see no water." This was a bizarre start to any discussion but it had to be pursued.

Uncomfortable at his boldness, I felt a malignancy in the offer. Maybe this was a part of my ongoing emergency, but beyond my comprehension.

"Sure there is," he said as he walked down the path and crossed the open ground.

How did I miss it? There was a collection of plants, bushes, fronds, and vines that crept up each other. Spreading some of these huge fronds, which were brown on the outside from the dust but were lush with color and vibrancy on the inner aspect. Thus with my visual field made whole again, I saw what was in front of me all along. There, surrounded on all sides by more tropical vegetation, was a gigantic lagoon. I could barely see its far shore. In places the vines hung over the waters, casting shapes on which one can imagine young boys swinging from and splashing into the waters below. Standing on a ledge, I appreciated the blue green turquoise waters lapping at my feet. Beams of sunlight pierced the water's clarity, and suspended particles reflected back its brilliance.

"I don't swim", I said.

"Don't worry, you won't drown."

So the coup de grace was to be delivered soon in a watery grave, I pondered. But how was he going to do me in? I was nervous; there was no exit, and my fate was sealed. Was I going to die again? Well, I thought, as long as I was dead there was no issue here but apprehension persisted.

"Will you come with me?" I asked.

"Sure," he answered. I felt a big splash as I pierced the water. It was cool and refreshing. I sensed another splash close by even as I felt myself going down, down and down. Air bubbles rose around me, they were going up, in the right direction; I was not. Close to panic, I pushed upward and soon broke the surface. I was floating and it was comfortable yet frightening as I could not see the bottom. My legs were clear in the transparent water but absorbed the colors of the water. They moved gently with no effort. Paddling slowly, I felt refreshed as the dust washed off me. I rubbed my torso enjoying the freshness that flowed over me and the water shed itself off my body and rolled down. My friend broke surface close, but not too close. He seemed to enjoy the jump as much as I did.

"Are you okay?"

"Yes," I answered, feeling more comfortable. Looking around me I saw we were in a secluded lagoon surrounded by thick bushes bearing huge frond-shaped leaves. There were isolated beaches where families were spending time together. They seemed preoccupied and not into mingling with others and didn't seem to notice my physical or mental manifestation. It was quiet, broken by the call of an occasional tropical bird that flew overhead in the azure skies that stretched from horizon to horizon. It was bright, yet I could not see the sun; the rays of light came somewhere from the firmament above, their origin hidden from me. I became more comfortable and adventurous with my new found floating and swimming skills. I felt now my companion was not going to do me in, but I still could not understand his presence. He seemed to know that he was a comfort to me. And thus I slowly moved across the waters enjoying its vigor and studying my new environment. It seemed so peaceful, bereft of negative human emotions, only tranquility. The families on the shore moved slowly, hesitatingly. They were in contrast to the environment they were in. Much later it dawned on me what I was witnessing. Others like me were transitioning from one world into another, here they were in limbo. Perhaps they were exchanging their last farewells. In the distance across the waters were others barely discernible. Curiosity was getting the better of me as I slowly headed in their direction. From a distance, it looked like two young boys were playing with fish as if they may have been house pets. There were certain resemblances that made me squint hard. They had made circles with their hands and the fish seemed to jump through these holes as the kids smiled and laughed.

"They look like my boys," I spoke.

"Possible," my friend answered.

"Can I swim to them?"

"Sure," he answered. It seemed a daunting task; I had to swim the whole breath of the lagoon across the deepest apart. Here the waters took on a dark hue that was not as inviting rather it made my task that much more daunting by taking on a menacing appearance; it was testing me, and I sensed the bottom was a long way down. Was this my undertaking I had to endure to escape my fate? Would I accept or throw in the towel right now .Without conscious volition I started my journey, thinking about it I would lose faith right away. My legs vanished in the swirls. Slowly my arms and legs propelled me toward them; the going was slow but methodical. I looked back a lot to see my friend, who kept pace with me. Neither did he encourage or dissuade me. What was his intent, and why did he keep me company? Not that I wanted him gone, rather I was comforted whenever I twisted around and he was there. It seemed that he was there exclusively for me and appeared content to let me lead the way.

Not having learnt to swim in the real world, I began to tire in a while. Slowing down I yet covered ground, even I was being drawn under. I vainly tried to stay propelled, yet my limbs became heavier and lost their ability to move on their own.

"I'm not going to make it."

"Slow down," he said. "You are going too fast. Take your time. Float awhile on your back." Was he talking about my life or the here and now? He showed me how, yet kept his distance from me. It took little time to master, and floating thus I rested for a while. Free of activity and supported by the water, my muscles loosened up again. The leaden feeling receded, blood circulated through cramped organs and eventually I could slowly resume my journey as my body regained its function and I propelled myself onwards again. I had a goal, and this lagoon was becoming a small challenge.

It was slow going and the thought of giving up crossed my mind repeatedly. Keeping my thoughts silent, I set out to finish my mission. There seemed no other meaningful task for me otherwise. In my musings I barely noticed the ripple moving toward me, until the waters but not two feet from me was pierced by the head of my youngest, Auti, as I then called him.

"Hi Dad, how you doing"? He asked.

"Austin, what are you doing"? I said, feeling the end was in sight.

"Wayne and me are playing with the fishes," he said pointing toward their location,

"Why don't you ask Wayne to come?" thinking the boys would help me to shore. At last there was going to be a quick reprieve, relief from my watery challenge. This was easy after all. As a child drowning was my worst form of death, it seemed unnecessarily painful and drawn out. Our neighbor had drowned in a beach incident, Hawkes Bay Beach, Karachi, Pakistan; gazing at his bloated features, water logged still haunts me. My sons, good swimmers were surely sent to rescue me from a similar fate. Ignoring me, his father, he dove back under the water and in what seemed a minute or two, was back at the shore playing with his brother. Did he not see I was close to drowning, what was he up to?

Well, this was a cruel joke. My confidence, survivability, and emotions plunged. I would have been angry if I was not so shocked and drained of all sentiment and left feeling even more vulnerable.

"Why did he do that?" Everyone seemed to know but me.

"Well your son is telling you that the position you're in is not where he wants to see his father, and in no uncertain terms he's telling you to move. He cannot help you but is impressing upon you he needs you on the other side. The decision and choice is yours, tough as it is; it is your choice. You are not in a safe setting and there is no room for debate."

That I could see, but the task seemed that much more challenging after being thrown a lifeline filled with hope and having it as quickly yanked away. Disheartened I continued my Herculean task. Resting for some time life and strength returned to me. Yet I was sapped, it was that much steeper from here on. Several times I felt like giving up, the waters enveloped me like amniotic fluid, nourishing, soothing, refreshing, wanting to hold me in its cocoon but my recent insight moved me against my own volition. My companion sensing my distraught state moved a tad closer but never so close that he was in arms reach."

"Take your time," he advised me. "You're moving too fast; rest awhile again"

"Will I make it?"

"Maybe."

Tunnel vision developed; I saw only the task at hand and slowly moved towards my goal. The beauty that had until recently so haunted me with its charm was full of venom. I saw nothing any more. After an eternity, I could discern facial characteristics on the boys. They were serene, happy, content playing with fish, which continued to play with them and seemed to like being scratched under their gills. I thought of the boys' pet at home, Tippy, a border collie-shepherd mix. I could not stop now. My muscles were tightening up again; this time they would not relax, they were knotted up and hardening with spasm, becoming more ineffectual with each passing moment. I was nearing the end of all my reserves, and I needed to rest again, not for too long now though. The boys were in plain sight and not too perturbed to see their dad coming nearer, and still they did not swim out a few yards to pull me in, even if my life depended upon it.

Excitement drove me forward, yet the frailty of my body kept my pace slow and measured. Progress was now measured in feet. My efforts were crumbling, yet my goal was inching closer. Wavelets were curling to the shore, splashing on me as they broke close by .Would I make it or was I doomed to a watery finale. Just as suddenly a rough texture rubbed against my toes, perhaps a fish or eel or serpent. There it was again this time I could dig a toe into it, yes it was the sandy bottom. Sinking, giving one last push off the bottom a few more feet were covered and I was now standing in neck high waters, my nostrils sucking in volumes of air, my chest heaving with exertion, lightheaded, I was too exhausted to savor the moment right that instant. It took a few minutes to recover and savor my triumph. And yet no recognition from my sons on my achievement although I was in plain sight and my ordeal was obvious. The waters had turned tranquil and see-through again, serenity descended on me, I could see the end of my journey was close.

"Those are my sons," I told my friend, trusting myself to finally speak again.

Was that a hint of a smile that I noticed? Yes it was, barely crinkling the corners of his mouth.

"Yes, they are."

Gosh, he wasn't one for long speeches. I still had not asked him who he was and why was he here with me. But the opportunity would arise, and soon all would be known.

As I slowly pushed myself the last few yards the waters receded from my torso, and not a minute too soon. Barely above the waves, resting on my hands and knees in a semi prostate existence, self-directed consciousness slowly reasserted itself. My head cleared, chest quit hurting, breathing steadily improved, muscles untwined themselves, vision got focused, I had done it!. The boys seemed unaware of my recent task yet and greeted me accordingly not too concerned. They knew their dad was going to make it all along; they had more faith in me than I had in myself and had reached out to pull me to safety. But the effort had to be mine, bittersweet as it had been.

"These are my sons." I turned to make introductions, (my parochial high school training had not left me) but my friend was not to be seen, only the slowly moving ripples that caressed the shore. The whole Polaroid of my recent adventure, its physical make up and its eclectic meaning imprinted upon my mind, this was my snapshot I carry with me always. I scanned the waters waiting to see a head bob up, but the scene was calm. Peace reigned; a few birds flew by looking at us and then flitted on to their destination.

"Boys, where is that chap who was beside me?"

"Dad, we don't see anyone else, you were by yourself!"

I faced the lagoon again even lonelier than before. My happiness was not whole, yet I was whole and home again.

"Thank you," I whispered. I had lost a companion but gained a friend. A bond had developed with someone and that would come back to guide me many times in the future. I felt someone touch my chest, it was exquisite, soft gentle. There was no discomfort, my heart was being massaged, and each beat got stronger with every caress. My coma was lifting; light was sensed on my eyelids. I opened my eyes to see my wife looking down at me.

Was I in a coma, or heavily sedated, or a combination of both? I tend to think it was the latter. I still have no desire to review my medical records. My feeling is that it may be too traumatic and may bring me closer to reliving the past, rather than to keep on moving in a new direction. I would one day like to look back at this calamity and see a purpose in it. I see many friends go through much more than I have and some-times feel fortunate. I had feeble chances of recovery from the outset, the initial insult was so massive, yet I was chosen to live through and survive such a ordeal. Physically I can now cycle fifteen miles (after my initial echo said my heart output was 15 percent, whereas a normal hearts output is closer to 70 percent, this meant that I was going to be an invalid all my life, a 'Cardiac Cripple'). Most heart patients in my condition develop problems within the first six months to two years. What ultimately disposes of patients like us is an irregularity in the heart beat called an arrhythmia. It is generated by diseased heart tissue and very often fatal. Thus in my case, not bad at all, I have survived three years with no major complication, it has to be a remarkable recovery of heart function and some muscle regeneration I am pretty bad at being a patient, not following up with my doctors as I should. However I had to have done something right to have come this far and to be productive and whole again .If I could do it so can others. Feel sorry for as long as you wish but only when the spark of preservation is lit and there is a purpose to fulfill will life get meaning again. There is nothing special about me that I survived. Divine intervention perhaps, good luck, also, maybe I paid for all my sins in one condemnation so I was set free again but with severe admonitions to do things differently, but I'm regular with my meds and many lifestyle changes and have prioritized my goals. Tune ups are frequent almost ongoing daily and thus always need to find a higher personal level of accountability.

What could I have done had I known such an event was going to occur? The word *kismet* that I take to mean that your life story is written indelibly on canvas the day you were born and that everything that happens is preordained. Was my event on March 3 preordained? Yes, and everything leading up to it. Everything! So I do find solace in this philosophy, which makes it easy to rationalize when you can't move forward because you are blaming yourself for mishaps, whether intentional or accidental. My kismet said the events would happen as they did.

3

LAST RITES

I was in an altered state, barely on the edge of consciousness. Some relief had descended on me; at least there was going to be a resolution—good or not, fatal or survival. Yet I was not going to be aware of what was to transpire. I was thankful that finally all would be known. I didn't care if I passed on, as this would also bring relief. The words in the ambulance were terse, pressured; lots of calls were made , much dialogue followed, considerably smeared. Speed slowed by bumps, a soft screech and more of the same. Very soon I entered a part of my existence that played a huge roll in my life and I wasn't even going to know what happened although I had better than a ringside seat.

My last recollection was of bumping over the threshold of the hospital, with cold air caressing me through every crevice of my blanket. Even as I almost passed out, I heard the last words I would hear for many days yet to come: "Guys, skip the emergency room. They want him up in the cath lab. The team is ready."

Ahh, relief. I could stop fighting as I passed out completely, unaware any more of my surroundings or proceedings. For some time going forward, I cannot recall what transpired however I have put together a collage of events in a credible sequence that would mimic what may have happened to me in the next crucial days. The rapid response at the receiving hospital was no doubt due to the phone calls made by my cardiologist friend. A team had been assembled in the late night hours and was ready for me on arrival. Most of what I document is from verbal encounters I had with friends, staff and well wishers. I refuse to review my records for various reasons. I don't feel I need to, as my thoughts are to remain fixed and that is how I would prefer it. Much time has passed, and I get more resistant to change.

Upon my arrival as my gurney bounced over the entrance lip of the accepting facility, the pace picked up dramatically. Here we have a middle-aged gentleman who a couple of hours ago was a functioning, high-output individual. Now here he was as nature intended: obtunded, unconscious, and at the precipice of life itself. The responsibility on the cath lab was tremendous. They had received a personal phone call. I needed to be saved, there was no alternative. The odds were not in their favor. I did not envy them their responsibility. They had probably had received word of my deteriorating status and impending doom. A heroic task awaited them, and they did a magnificent job.

I would have rocked in the stretcher as I was rushed to the cath lab. That I didn't go to the ER first showed how concerned they were on identifying the blockage in my heart blood vessel and opening it as soon as possible. The rush was on to rescue the heart muscle that was damaged and rapidly dying. The doors would have opened with a voice command or the touch of a finger. Quickly strong arms would have gathered me up transferring me from the gurney to the procedure table. The IV bags would have been passed over, secured to permanent poles. The devices attached to my chest would have been reconnected, and the tangle of tubes and wires straightened and put in their respective places. Bright lights would have bathed my torso, while around the table would have been a penumbra. My chest was shaved (I saw what they had done later. Quite nice, but not up to spa standards.) in anticipation of various devices placed on my chest, included a defibrillator in case my heart beat became so irregular they would have to shock me. If it was used, it might leave burn marks on my chest (there weren't any. I checked later). My groin was shaved. Even as my loss of consciousness made me lose all sense of modesty, it would not have mattered. With a blood pressure as low as mine, there would be a frantic attempt to put fluids into my veins to raise it. Powerful meds like dopamine would have been started to help raise my BP. Sterile medical devices would have been ripped from their vacuumed plastic bags, in anticipation of their emergent use.

My new cardiologist (thank God doctors can function deep into their R.E.M. sleep time) while coordinating the grand orchestra, would have expediently gained access to my heart with a device introduced into my groin. There piercing the skin it would have been pushed into a artery and then with great skill been threaded upwards into another blood vessel called the aorta. Now going against the flow of blood it would continue to snake upwards until it reached the point where the heart and blood vessel met. It has now reached the point where with extraordinary skill the blood vessels that actually supply the heart muscle is investigated. The primary job would have been to determine the location of the obstruction, if it could be fixed in the heart lab, or if I would need open heart surgery. (There was no zipper on my chest when I awoke. Whew!) Being unconscious, I would have cooperated as they draped and exposed vitals body sites. I would not have felt the initial poke as the wire was threaded through to my heart. Then various catheters helped my doc search for the obstruction, even as my vital signs deteriorated, indicating the severity of the emergency and a need for urgency at a higher level.

To find out precisely where the obstruction is in the heart the catheter is sequentially placed in several blood vessels supplying the heart muscles. A small amount of dye that is compatible with human tissue would have been squirted into each vessel consecutively. Special cameras over my chest would take very rapid pictures of my heart. Slowly the images would reveal the obstruction. Next came the big question: could I be treated by a stent? This is a small, hollow device that is delicately placed at the site of the obstruction and gently expanded to flatten the obstruction against the wall of the blood vessel, letting the blood flow again to heart muscles starved of oxygen and nutrients. Or would I need open heart surgery? If there were multiple blockages. If the obstruction was in certain locations, surgery would give me a better outcome. Of course this would mean stepping up the ante and was I competent enough medically to stand the rigors of open heart surgery.

All this information is processed on the fly. It requires a lot of expertise and prodigious multitasking. I presumed the procedure itself was straight forward enough, yet my vital signs were severely compromised, requiring multiple medical interventions to sustain me until the obstruction was relieved and the heart could pump again with any degree of efficiency . This would determine if I lived or died. If the former would I be a cardiac cripple or would I lead a productive life. I was told later that I was given multiple fluid boluses to fill up my blood vessels and raise my blood pressure.

Another medication, Dobutamine, would have been started to help raise my BP. I knew multiple interventions had been done because when I awoke there were multiple puncture marks of a large caliber on my extremities. There was certainly a fight on. Fluids were pouring into my body while powerful medications were dripping into me trying to tighten my blood vessels and support my pressure. The heart specialist was doing her utmost to localize my blockage, all the while paying attention to the monitors and displays that showed my condition worsening.

Since unconsciousness had swept over me, I have no knowledge of what was happening. I could definitely say there was more sweat on the team working on me than on myself. In fact my skin would have been dry and cool, eyelids closed, motionless, my torso and limbs aligned so that access could be obtained to various locations for various reasons. A Foley catheter would have been placed in my bladder to ensure my urinary output was adequate. There would be a manual blood pressure cuff on my left arm. There probably would have been a sanitized gown draped over my lower torso with a fenestration for easy access to the cut down or surgical sites. I would be left still so as not to blur the images.

One of the problems when the heart does not beat strongly is that blood pools in certain locations upstream or behind from the heart. The lungs are first to feel the pressure that is built up. As the backup increases fluid pools into the lungs, literally flooding them. On the monitor, a low oxygen level would start an alarm. Normal oxygen saturation is around 98 percent or greater. If the level drops below 95 percent, oxygen would have been administered to the lungs via certain flexible tubes placed in the nostrils. Below 90 percent, a mask may have been placed over the mouth and nose, and oxygen would have been pushed in by a pressure system. Below 80 percent, the patient gets a breathing mask with a seal so that a higher concentration of oxygen would have been pushed with even greater force down into the lungs.

Oxygen saturation, rate of breathing, and other factors would have been taken into consideration as to how the patient was responding to the therapy and adjusted accordingly. A worsening of the oxygen level would indicate further fluid buildup in the lungs and, by inference, a worsening of the heart function. Should the status deteriorate further, a tube is inserted through the mouth, down the throat (overcoming a powerful gag reflex), into the main breathing tube going on to divide and supply both the lungs. This tube is hooked to a ventilator, a pump that pushes a certain amount of air enriched with oxygen into the lungs. The ventilator is a remarkable device yet is quite a dummy. Programmed properly it will push a predetermined amount of air into the lungs. It does this at a steady rate, with a certain volume, under a certain pressure, to ensure delivery of the oxygen. Too much or too little of any of these parameters and catastrophe ensues within. This could include shifting of the lungs, compression or even worse a tear in the lungs causing a entirely new set of problems.

Doreen told me when I was wheeled out of the suite I was on a ventilator . Thus indeed I had worsened over the last few hours. Really a herculean task was done in rescuing me in the wee hours of the night. It had been less than 10 hours since I first had my symptoms and I had gone through quite an ordeal already. I was unconscious, on life support; vital signs were in the toilet. In some circumstances my medications were maxxed out. Now it was up to me to turn around to start responding to the interventions that were carried out. Time was critical, the sooner I responded the better were my chances of a robust recovery, which was what everyone was hoping for. As it seemed right now my a nightmare was unfolding. A normal cath lab procedure would have taken about an hour from the time it started to being rolled out to the recovery suite. I had been there for about six hours. This had been a mighty battle.

More recently they have started doing this procedure [cardiac catherization] from the wrist, shortening the length of catheter needed and thereby reducing chances of complications and cleaning up the procedure field. Although this procedures has it detractors it may be the procedure of the future. Once the obstruction was localized again, a similar algorithm would be followed about the best way to treat the patient. Doctors would determine what type of intervention would be used. Although fraught with complications, this procedure is quite safe thanks to the intense training of doctors in this field.

As I left the catheterization lab at eight thirty the next morning this was my scenario. First I was rolled to the CCU intensive care unit. I was on a breathing machine, silently its bellows pushed vital oxygen into my lungs trying to keep a high enough level in my blood to nourish my tissues, allowing them to continue the complicated biological procedures that keep us alive. It was a difficult job. My lungs were flooded with fluids blocking the uptake of oxygen. My body was very deprived. At what level does the brain start to fail? When do the measurements of brain activity start to falter? How long before the damage is considered irreversible? When does one see the bright light beyond? I didn't care to find out, even if the answers were available.

Along with the ventilator I was hooked to powerful heart stimulants that were flogging it to continue to pump as vigorously as possible under the circumstances. The alternative was not acceptable. The combination was powerful and used only in the most critical situations.

Fluids would be forced in via large needles buried in my veins to help keep the blood flowing. A drug called Levophed is used in last-ditch efforts. Its catchphrase is, "Leave 'em dead." I was for some time on the highest dose possible; however my blood pressure remained in the sixties. In spite of all these meds and fluids, this BP was life threatening in itself. Yet in my circumstance, while in the cath lab, a balloon pump was inserted into a big vessel near my heart. This expanded and shrunk in juxta sequence to my heart trying to keep the blood pressure up. These efforts were thwarted by my situation. I can only imagine the rivulets of cold sweat bathing the staff in the lab as they struggled. Now they had to deal with my collapsed cardiac status.

Nobody wants to work on an unstable patient. That's why doctors do a preoperative consult, to identify and remove any factors that could make the surgery risky. But my team had no choice. The human element would have been very real in the lab. My procedure took six hours. The team sweated over me from about two to eight in the morning. Talk about a red-eye procedure. Their rest was more than justly earned, but I imagine they would check in with me about every ten minutes, wondering if their toils would falter or if I would arise again.

And yet I was blissfully unaware. When did my vision start, I was in a coma, blessedly unaware, for five days. For three of them, I was on the "he probably won't make it" list. Why do I say that? My wife tells me that shortly after emerging from the lab, someone asked her if we practiced any faith. She told the person that we were Catholics. This person thought it would be beneficial for me to receive the last rites, a ritual common to many religions in different forms. In Catholicism, it a sacrament administered by the priest to an individual who is near death or in danger of dying. It helps prepare family and friends for a loved one's departure. It also alerts anyone who may be concerned that, although we pray for divine intervention, the body is only the vessel that carries the soul, which is being called back to its maker. Knowing that our loved one is going to meet St. Peter soon makes us feel that we have to give up our selfish desires of wanting to possess a loved one and that we have to give in to "the circle of life" [which is a phrase from a well-known children's movie that I cherish; it was the first movie I took my eldest son to alone, when he was less than three. It was a boys night out]. The spiritual ritual makes the inevitable understandable and gives the living a platform from which to grieve for the departed.

A priest came in that morning to my bedside. He would have stood by me saying solemn prayers making the unofficial announcement that I was probably not going to make it. My wife later related that devout as she was, it was not in her comprehension that her husband might not survive. Perhaps I would put it down to fatigue of staying awake all night and the incredible rapidity of events that proceeded.

As I was wheeled into my ICU room, Doreen noticed that there were two nurses assigned to me. In a normal ICU room it is normally one nurse to one or two patients at the most. The more critical the situation the more likely that it would be one on one. And yet to have two nurses assigned to care for me highlighted my precarious situation. There was so much gadgetry attached to me that monitoring everything would have been too much for one nurse. The heart medicines would have been regulated closely, IV fluids would have flowed in. My body would have been repositioned frequently to avoid bedsores. The balloon pump inserted around my heart would have a sophisticated pump attached to it on the outside. The two parts would have met at my groin, this one on the left side, the point of insertion of the device as it threaded up to its location. My lungs had a breathing tube inserted within just at a critical point in my airway, on the outside a respirator programmed to my size and many other parameters would be doing its job unfailingly with a muffled "whoosh" and soft moaning's. This would have been monitored by a respiratory technician. Secretions from my mouth would have been suctioned to prevent them dribbling into my lungs, due to a suppressed gag reflex. To monitor my kidney functions, my urinary output would have been monitored as well. A respiratory therapist would have monitored my ventilator settings to make sure I was getting enough oxygen and air, and to check my oxygen level in my blood. The breathing tube would have been taped to my mouth. Its position inside my body is vital—too far in or not far enough could compromise my breathing, or what was left of it.

I precariously clung to life. My blood pressure was in the toilet; my oxygen level wouldn't have sustained a salamander. This is what ICU staff call a slow code. Death was almost inevitable. My wife hovered around and later told me that she felt lost and overwhelmed. Much of what she was told was too technical. There was a hollow feeing in the pit of her stomach. Yet she still did not appreciate the seriousness of the matter.

Doreen had texted my brother, whose number was handy, and he spread the news rapidly to siblings, mother, cousins, in laws, well-wishers, old friends back home, and other friends who had emigrated from Pakistan to other parts of the world over the last twenty-five years.

My wife was overwhelmed by the number of calls she received and either declined a lot or has no remembrance of the people she spoke to. Most went unanswered due to the sheer number. My extended family was further inundated with more calls. As my mom and siblings arrived, there was confusion about how sick I really was. Many messages had flown back and forth, and the message was that Conrad was in the hospital ICU having suffered a heart attack, but was making a recovery. What my family saw confounded their senses. How could this happen to Conrad? He was comatose, unresponsive, hooked up to many IVs, a tube sticking out of his mouth, maybe a Foley catheter in place. Obviously, he was very sick. But how? Why? Less than half a day ago he had spoken to some of us and nothing seemed amiss. So fast, so sick. It was very quiet as they contemplated my body swathed in a white hospital gown. They prayed silently for me. There were no cries or moaning. I still had a chance.

The doctors reassured the family that I would be okay in spite of how critical I seemed. They noticed that there was no spontaneous activity and I was nonresponsive to stimuli. Some of them wondered if I was thinking or if that was possible in a coma. And word spread even more. The calls quadrupled. A few of the local groups from back home on the internet offered their prayers and condolences. That first day, many were wondering about Doreen and how she and the boys were holding up. However my wife was only concerned about my condition and thoughts in the "post-me" period had not entered her head.

My sons came to visit every evening. On the initial visit Wayne, my eldest, a reserved and serious young man, introspective yet witty, broke down on the waiting room couch, where he put his head in his arms and sobbed forever. His uncles consoled him yet he kept his thoughts to himself and sobbed. He later said he was feeling lost and afraid for the future. My younger one seemed more confused. Maybe it was too unreal for him. I wonder what they will remember when in their forties. My sons went to school, taken by my staff and friends. Even on the first day, their friends asked them if it was true, was their dad in the hospital? Word had gotten out that fast.

With calm understatement they later recalled that they knew I would be alright from the beginning. Why? Because I was hooked up to so much technology that there was no way I would not make it. We all have our defense mechanisms and as this was what the boys clung to, the faith in technology, it was also to be noted that their lives revolved within this new world. It [technology] was only on the fringes of my life till then.

Being in the medical profession back home as matter of the morning news report, it was texted that I was transported in critical condition to a nearby hospital with a serious heart problem. The staff at most doctors' offices and others knew of my status by lunch. I was the talk of the town, and I didn't even know it. My office that morning was flooded with calls from concerned patients, other doctors' offices wanting confirmation, asking for further updates information, offering condolences. Many left their numbers and asked to be called right away if there was any change. Many visitors came; ironic, I thought later, as I myself shy away from hospital visits. To me it reminds me of work, and just by looking at the meds flowing, I feel being back in the driver's seat.

At the hospital my breathing status steadily deteriorated, I was breathing rapidly, wheezing, chest muscles expanding and contracting, saliva drooling out of the corner of my mouth, with small bubbles within. I was fighting the breathing tube that connected me to the ventilator. It entered my body through my lips, pushed my tongue down, and came to rest about three inches from the neck notch. As my lungs were congested with fluid, this acted as a barrier for air to enter and leave all leading to a very low oxygen level in my blood. A friend relates later how he would see my muscles rapidly twitching, a sign of the brain getting irritated, and this could have led to frank seizures if matters were not reversed. My oxygen saturation with all the interventions was still in the fifties. That was extremely bad and could not sustain me much longer without serious organ damage and soon death of key body parts. Something would give if not corrected and yet everything was being done. I was actually in an ongoing code.

Many friends in the medical profession came to visit. One was noted to remark in the waiting room that I would not make it. This was picked up by one of my brothers and caused great consternation. Of course it was obvious looking at my stats on the monitors the writing was on the wall.

Then my next miracle happened. A good friend and physician visited me. In one glance he would have taken in the whole scene, and nothing would have missed his keen eye. Believe me; I have seen this man in action. His knee jerk reaction to my low oxygen level led him to put a stethoscope on my chest. He soon saw something that no one else had seen. He asked my wife for approval to see my chest X-ray and demanded to see it right away. This was promptly put up on the fluorescent screen, and immediately his fears were confirmed. The breathing tube had slipped into my right airway leaving not enough air to keep my left lung inflated. The left lung had collapsed, worsening the breathing capacity and thus causing some of my problem. Immediately the staff was informed and the tube was repositioned. But my lung failed to respond and stayed collapsed. Then a respiratory specialist was summoned. Promptly I was scheduled for a washing of my lungs (bronchoscopy). The goal was to flush out any mucus that might have been blocking the airway and let it expand. This was done that evening with all expediency. The procedure went by as best as can be expected given my precarious situation. Some secretions were removed from my lungs, but no obstructions were found.

Something that had happened during my coma was that I had a suppressed gag reflex. That would have made clearing my throat difficult and saliva would have dribbled into my lungs.

That caused pneumonia, which X-rays were now showing in both lungs. So we had a collapsed lung and a double pneumonia and a congestive heart failure that flooded my lungs with fluid. Thus I progressed through the night, unstable and in critical condition. Realistically my odds of survival were less than 10 percent and falling. Perhaps my odds for those several critical days were closer to nonexistent.

The next morning blood work revealed that my blood count was low. The hemoglobin level was low. I was leaking blood from somewhere. Further tests showed I had an ulcer or severe stomach irritation that caused what is called a GI bleed. Though unlikely, it but quite possible, I was on many blood thinners that could have made me bleed that much easier. So now the blood bank found a match for my blood type and a transfusion was started. I finally ended up receiving three units of blood. This also helped to increase my blood pressure by a notch, but every bit helped.

Lots of visitors came by. Doreen had been there the previous night and into the day. Seems I was a jerking a bit too much and at times her words piercing through my semi-comatose state seemed to reach me, and my body didn't spasm that much.

My family took turns to make sure my wife was not alone. Many times she was reassured that I would be okay, and was advised to go home and rest.

"No, my place is by my husband," she would say. She would eat at the cafeteria or sustenance others brought in for her. My sons returned that evening. Surrounded by their cousins they kept their sobs within. Austin, my youngest, passed out so fast after seeing me again his head could be heard hitting the floor. None the less he was quickly revived with water and juices. I didn't ask him if he had a headache after the incident when I eventually found out.

My family did not tell me much about how I was during my coma. At first I felt they were to trying to protect me from what was a tumultuous event, but later I felt that there was so much information and conflicting stories that it was not possible for one layperson to take it in and regurgitate it later, much less make sense of it all. My wife was too emotional to take in the complexity; she was concerned that her husband needed to survive. There were two young boys who needed me as well. It was a critical time in their lives. They were going through puberty and the teenage years. Grades had to be maintained and long-term plans discussed. Alas, neither of them were interested in the medical field as a career. I myself have bittersweet thoughts about the medical profession. Bad as it was becoming, so that saving a patient's life will come down to resources that are being squandered away.

As the second day drew to a close, I had a double pneumonia, a collapsed left lung, bleeding from my stomach, a liver in shock, kidneys that were on the verge of failing, and a brain that, well, I'm not sure how to describe. Was it dead? Was it so dysfunctional that it was temporarily fried, unable to process information and react to keep the body in harmony? Or was it in limbo waiting for a signal to come back to life or fade away abandoning the soul to go to its appointed place? I think I came as close as ever to finding out. Any further and I would know the true story of creation, and if St. Peter really was at the pearly gates of heaven.

What strikes me is that after waking up, I felt the most rested I have ever felt in spite of the blows my body endured. Something or somebody was protecting me from the horrors unfolding around and within me. One thing I wish I could have done was to be able to contact my wife during the coma and reach her in a telepathic or spiritual manner, so I could have been with her through her struggles.

Through the evening, visitors kept streaming through; I hope I was appropriately covered. However if not it's not something I feel embarrassed about. That evening after my wife had brought the boys home, she was having a cup of tea and received a call from my friend Sunit, the physician who discovered my collapsed lung. He brought Doreen up to speed on my situation. It could not have been a task he relished, yet he did what needed to be done. Making the language simple he summarized what had and was happening to me and that I was in a critical condition, really critical. He related choking as he talked with my wife, clearly being such close family friends had affected his composure. Being a stoic Doreen had blocked what could really happen and had kept a stiff upper lip, upto now. Her composure failed, and she collapsed. Reality sank in; her husband was very sick and fragile. His chances of recovery were slim to none. She put her head in her hands and sobbed. Wayne sat beside her and held her as they both cried away. She told the boys how it was possible that their father might not make it, and she had no idea how to live without me. That was the closest the family had ever been. Raw emotions and tears flowed freely She further thought to herself how to raise the boys without me. However by ten that night she was back by my side. She had kept the discussion to herself stoically.She had decided not to relate to the others her recent discussion and kept her vigil by my side.

Often she was distracted into taking a break, refreshments, and naps, but she refused to leave my side. She slept on the couch in my room courtesy of the staff, who understood her overdrive, and that nothing was to be done but support her. Wistfully she dozed through the night waking up whenever monitors beeped or the staff intervened.

My vitals did not deteriorate any further. That would have been terminal. Officially I continued to remain unresponsive, but at this time I had an experience that some might describe as out-of-body. I had heard of many such stories and to that point never made much of such thoughts. My very brief experience did not affect me much, yet in that small period along with my dream was the closest I have felt to being on the other side. I felt on a certain night I was perched high in one corner of the room near the ceiling on a ledge. It was obvious no one seemed to know of my presence, gazing down at my wife; her upper torso lay on the bed; her hand lay on mine. She was asleep, her body slowly moving with her breathing. I saw myself motionless on the bed, my head was twisted up and to the left, a breathing tube pushed air into my lungs at a steady rate causing my chest to move.

One of my many sisters-in-law was on the other side, rubbing my arm. Staff quietly circled as they discharged their heavy duties. Yet all was quiet and peaceful, nothing to cause concern or anxiety. It felt reassuring. I don't know why, but I felt this experience happened on this night.

And then the image closed. I recollect no more. I drifted into a special space for which we have no scientific explanation, only spiritual and religious ones. In the wee hours of that morning I spiked a temperature of 104 degrees Fahrenheit. That meant a new infection had developed.

Most likely with so many IV lines and foreign objects in my body I had developed line sepsis. This could happen given all the interventions happening to me. Thus my antibiotics were changed and a new ingredient was introduced into the soup. Yet my vitals stayed stable, no worsening. That following morning the word was cautious but on the positive side. Several members of the family went home to catch up on their lives, which they had let slide during this period. But yet there was always someone with my wife. The boys were attended by friends, my office staff, and family. They opted to continue going to school and came to visit every evening. Often I wondered what they endured.

My vitals came up by about 10 points on all counts later that day. My blood pressure had come, pulse had slowed down, oxygen level up, skin color good, urinary output brisk and more spontaneous movement on my side There was hope that I would make it. To my friends word spread that I was doing better. To those in the field knowing how my vitals had changed indicated my organs were recovering from the assault of the previous days. They had started to function but just barely. Many things could go wrong, but for the moment it was good.

My wife sensed the slight elation of my nurses and, though unable to comprehend the numbers, felt the slight levity of spirit. That evening she went home briefly and, with some guilt, tells the story of how laid her head down for a nap awoke the next morning. Exhaustion had caught up with her and the sleep had rested her body and senses. No dreaded phone calls from the hospital to shatter the peace. I behaved myself in the room. My vitals didn't alarm as much, and as early morning came I seemed to have a peaceful countenance about me.

My wife returned to my side as soon as the boys were dropped off to school. Though still not responsive, my vitals continued to improve. After some tests, it was decided to try taking me off the breathing machine. I breathed on my own after initially choking as the tube removal tickled my throat. My vitals indicated a small strengthening of the heart causing the blood pressure to come up to life sustaining levels. The strong stimulants were slowly decreased and as no untoward incident occurred over the next several hours they were stopped. There was a complex soup of chemicals within me that also further suppressed brain function and they had to wear off. Later that evening my wife reported that I was vaguely responsive for brief seconds and then would drift off into a semi-comatose state. The next day I seemed to turn my head to track voices briefly yet without comprehension.

I really wish I could have remembered some of my thoughts at this time. There is a feeling that when I returned to the present world, a decision was made that I would be allowed to live with mortals like myself again. Yet there would be certain trials I would have to endure in my new world, tests that would be even greater than what I had endured, but they would be of a different nature—a test of my spirit, my soul, my intellect. If

I had a choice, in retrospect I would have preferred to stay in the coma for another year or infinity. There would be no coincidental traveler or a good Samaritan to guide me, or perhaps there was, and I am unable to see him. Perhaps I still have not reached a state of understanding that would open new visions to me. Perhaps I never will.

The next morning matters remained stable. I was actually trying to open my eyes when called. I was moving more, and had to be told to lie still. There were still too many needles in me. My wife relates that I was responding with ever greater vigor. My eyes were opening but not focused. My level of consciousness kept on rising but I was not yet responding to the external world. I drifted into another deep sleep. It was afternoon later that day when I finally awoke in a fully conscious state. There wasn't a period of orientation. I woke up fully cognizant of my surroundings. I felt rested, like I'd had a very deep afternoon nap on an Indian summers day. My skin was sensitive; it felt the air resting against me. My gown gently caressed my hairs, I felt quite well. Ahhh, I thought, the procedure went well. I feel terrific. Good I'll go home soon and resume work. And then my wife's face entered my field of vision. She looked at me wondering and worried. I looked back amused.

"Are you awake?"

"Yes."

"Where are you?"

"At the hospital."

And from there we continued on. After that dialogue, my elation collapsed, my goodwill evaporated, horrific feelings raced through me. Am I that ill? How could I feel that well in spite of what had happened? And I dropped off into a deep slumber again, peaceful. I recollected my vision and willed myself to go back to that world, but it was for naught. I woke up later that evening. Other family members were present, and I discerned familiar voices. I was asked if I was thirsty. Yes, I was.

"What would you like?"

"A diet Pepsi, Cold." Coma or not, I needed my fix. I got that quickly enough and it was wonderful trickling down my throat, refreshing my parched membranes. The familiar comfortable flavor was never so refreshing. I sipped and slurped that beverage. It chilled me, refreshed me and most of all had welcomed me back to the material world, letting me know I was alive. I was in hog heaven just with one soda! Everyone was giving me so much attention.

"What else?',

"Coffee, cream and sugar?"

That drink also materialized shortly. Being hot, a straw was used to suck that beverage. It felt hot yet so good and refreshing, bringing back comfortable feelings just the same as the soda.

The next morning I continued to improve. Feeling up to it, I swung my legs off the bed to use the facilities. My head spun, the ground wobbled, my arms were lifeless and had no strength. A queasy feeling hit my guts. Vision took on a gray tinge. Maybe I should fall back on the bed. My wife came to my rescue aiding me. Drenched in sweat I rested, the room slowly settled down and righted itself. I had no strength or muscle tone to support me. I should have known better. Resting for some time but refusing to give up ,I tried once again. I sat on the edge of the bed for some time and sipped liquids. I gently arose, wobbly, the proverbial knees knocked together. I held on to my wife this time I stayed upright. Then the enormity of my predicament descended upon me. I was physically whopped. 7 days with no spontaneous movement had drained me of all my strength. I was completely deconditioned. Could I Have become that weak. Looking forward partial or complete recovery was a long ways off. Was I up to it.

I was screwed. Implications raced through my mind. How would I keep my practice covered? There were many bills to be paid, and I wasn't on top of my finances. There was a new car we had bought, some projects were in the pipeline, and the economy in our area had tanked. Once we were among the most enviable place to invest and in one year there was a feeling that things were not going as the pundits had predicted. Owners of homes were foreclosing in record numbers, the bankruptcy courts were swamped. So many people could not hold on, businesses were folding all around us. Homes and businesses built at the top of the housing boom could not sustain their expenses and were defaulted on or remained vacant causing further bankruptcies.

This was the setting in which I found myself now. Never did I think it would get this bad. This was a personal black swan event—totally unexpected and one that would change us for life.

A friend visiting with me told me to apply for disability as it was going to be a long time before I returned to work, if ever I did. Couched in kind words he was telling me I would never be able to work again. I had to change the paradigm of my life and move on with my new restrictions. Could I accept such a fate, forty eight years of age and unable to work!. I would not be able to live with myself. Rotting and withering away seemed more like it. Right there and then I made a fateful decision; I could not, would not live like this. Everything I had learnt, every challenge I had faced had taught me a thing or two from the past. I would refocus myself on the upcoming battle and proverbially die trying or make it no matter how long it took. I was going to, had to change my priorities. I did a mental calculation and, yes, I did have some breathing time. I would make it work.

There were so many things to think about that my mind was incoherent. Could I take a time out? I am supposed to rest after a heart attack like mine for up to six months. Long nights of sleep, no stress or responsibilities, lots of healthy activity, healthy meals, mental regrouping, afternoon naps, and a revised plan of what my new goals would be and redefine what work I could and could not do. It would take some time for me to find out how much I would recover. My heart was functioning at 20 percent of predicted capacity, not sustainable for daily activity. I would be a cardiac cripple, bouts of frequent hospitalizations for congestive heart failure, irregular heart rate requiring a defibrillator and a pacemaker. Be that as it may, I was going to move foreward to reconstruct myself. Most importantly I would show my boys that dad could do it and perhaps be an example for them should they face major calamities in their own lives down the road.

My head rang with my thoughts as they reverberated through me. Finally I slept deeply overcome with mental exhaustion. In the morning I awoke on a different floor. My recovery had started. Breakfast was nourishing, even as I noted the bland diet. I asked if I could go home. I was living up to the reputation that medical professionals made bad patients, yet I suppressed my curiosity and did not ask what meds I was receiving or what my vitals were.

Today I got to studying my body. My groin was very interesting. It was black and blue. Two lumps the size of kiwis were on either side, no doubt the site where all the catheters were inserted. From the size of all the bruising, they had apparently been working on me for a long time. I really should find out who that doctor was and send her flowers.

There were skin pressure ulcers on the back of my thighs. How did that happen? There were a few puncture wounds around my ankles. They needed a lot of sites to give me all those meds simultaneously. My chest was wickedly shaved, I didn't smell burning hair so that meant at least they did not have to shock me. Electrical leads were hooked to the bare spots that ran to monitors. My upper and lower arms on both sides were pin cushions. Most of the catheters were out, yet a reminder of their use persisted.

On the roof of my mouth there was a huge crater, my tongue flicked the margins of the ulcer where loose skin was hanging, no doubt caused by the friction of the tube that was placed in my lungs. My lips were bruised, swollen with tiny exquisite cuts. My throat was sore. It was painful to swallow, making it difficult to keep up my nutrition. There were some scars on my neck. Now what were they doing up there—more IV access?. My muscles seemed like the consistency of putty, no doubt lack of use and inability to keep up with nutrition and the high metabolic rate my condition had put me in had catabolized them. They were so ineffectual I had to concentrate on just taking a few steps at a time. The lack of oxygen and other vital nutrients had muddled up my brain. Inadequate chemical transmitters were making communication and coordinating with different muscle groups a challenge. For a moment I felt like a baby taking his first steps. Yet sheer stupidity would not let me give in. My instinct for survival and self-preservation would not let me down. Having faced many, many challenges in my life, participating in competitive sports and others I had too much (that is, pride) would not let me quit. I wanted to live, survive, and finish my life to its expected expectancy. I came from a background of fighters.

My family name is Castellino. Back home in Pakistan, my parents, brothers, and sister were all outstanding. None of us was a quitter. We had risen from extremely humble beginnings to what we were today. We were not from the elite of our community. But to take on a Castellino in school, play, studies, or anything was not a light undertaking. My father a simple man had distinguished himself as a man with significant accomplishments to his credit. The family was large, resources were scarce, but our brains and minds were more powerful than many others. We didn't have laurels we could rest on. We were trend setters, challenging the establishment back home, upsetting the apple cart and it was just a matter of time before we established ourselves, seven brothers and one sister, not one a quitter, alone we were good, together we were great feeding off each other's accomplishment.

In school at St. Patrick's High, when my name was called on the first day of a class, the teacher invariably asked, "Are you the brother of so and so?"

"Yes, I am."

Then I was studied up and down. No doubt the teacher was remembering another Castellino in her class. Was this one of the same caliber? Would he perform? How could such a large family with such limited resources keep putting out superstars? What made them different?

Being among the youngest, I was always hearing stories about the accomplishments of my brothers, and at times it was overwhelming. One story I remember vividly was about my eldest brother. In high school a teacher was talking about advanced algebra, first day. My brother was not paying attention and in fact was reading a novel. He was scolded severely and then to be ridiculed was pulled to the black board to solve a problem. Without any hesitation, my eldest brother took the chalk and without even a blink had written the solution on the board as he was being chewed out. Wish I could have been there. The teacher was going to make a monkey out of him. The haranguing continued until the teacher turned around saw the problem had been solved. A legend grew that here was a bunch of bright kids, and you better know your stuff before picking on them.

Much later in life, at Yosemite National Park, near where I used to work, my brothers were vacationing in remote spots. On separate occasions my brothers recalled my name being hollered at them. They turned around to see a stranger who was looking for me. My brothers said that, yes, Conrad is their brother and we do look alike. In conversation many pleasantries were exchanged as my patients related how they knew me and complimented my brothers on the care they had received from me. I seemed to be not of the mold that doctors were supposed to be. There was a cosmic thread running through all of this. I was asked back home if I was their brother and now the compliment was returned; Fascinating.

I was the wildest of the lot, yet like the others had a tremendous capacity for punishment and could still keep going. With this as my heritage, I could not let myself down. I was going to rise from the ashes once again. Self-pity, remorse, stupidity, and a blown out heart were not going to stop me. I will be vindicated, but I had to undertake the journey. There were going to be insurmountable hurdles. Maybe I should quit now, file for disability, go live with my wife's family, and wait until my life was done, which was not going to be long given my present condition. A heart beating at only 20 percent efficiency was asking for too many complications perhaps more suited for a medical textbook. Life expectancy was highly limited. Yet I was too mule-headed to know the game was over. *Khattam* (Urdu). Checkmate.

I drifted in and out of restful slumber again. My wife rested on my arm, a computer on her lap. She was replying to emails concerning me.

When I awoke next, my next angel had arrived. Doreen's eldest sister, Marlu had flown in to help take care of me and help out my wife. My first shower was an event of heroic proportions, I was breathless in the stream, my legs trembled, my heart beat harder, yet I was refreshed, clean, but short of breath and exhausted. My feelings of despair crawled over me again. And I saw my sister-in-law studying my countenance; she was sizing up the situation and planning her strategy. That day I reluctantly got my doctor to agree to discharge me the next morning. Deep inside, I was afraid of going home. At least here I was monitored 24/7. A wonderful nurse who had cared for me wished me the best. I wish I had kept her name somewhere. Of course there were many others most who I didn't know.

4

HOMECOMING

The next day was tremulous. My hospital stay was over. As bad as it was, while I was comatose I was shielded from the trauma that wracked my body mentally and physically until finally I woke up. The recent past was still surreal, and when I woke up in the morning I tried to will it away but to no avail. It was there to stay and to overpower my thoughts and actions for perhaps the rest of my life. Already as the past was to govern my future I tried to find courage, to summon strength for the battle to come. Little did I know I was already defeated but had not surrendered, too stupid again. I had to keep on doing what I did best and what had sustained my family for the last twenty years. Sitting on my butt for the rest of my life would leave me with no self-respect—not what I expected of myself. I could not live with no expectations.

As I stepped into the car the natural fragrance of the air never smelled so good. As the car rolled, so did my stomach. I was having motion sickness. Yet as we continued, the ride eased my nerves and I surveyed the same highway I had recently traveled in much different straits. Reaching home, I was refreshed by the comfortable odors, colors, textures, and furniture. Everything was spit polished. The old sofa was never so inviting as I stretched out my tired limbs. They seemed so frail, and so there was going to be a lot of recuperation in my future. I lay down and idle chatter let me fall gracefully into sleep. I was doing a lot of that recently, sleeping, it was deep yet not too long in duration but restorative. I was comfortable for now. My sister-in-law seemed to know how to care for really sick individuals. Every time I awoke I had to take some nourishment. None of the white folk's food. There were chapattis with chicken curry, raita on the side. There was pulao rice with fish masala. Not that I could eat much; even a child's portion was enough. My stomach rumbled at its first tasty was and sustaining meal in a long time. It felt euphoric and satiated. My gut distended and relaxed. Everything was forgotten. Looking back, I realized that the comfort of foods from childhood, eaten with friends and family and celebrating past events, nurtured oneself in trying times.

The phones were turned down low, their incessant ringing begging for attention. Well-wishers, family, friends, and acquaintances wanted to stay abreast of the latest health bulletin. Flowers were there by the bouquets, all on the antique reproduction table.

"Who are they for?" I asked.

"You, of course," Doreen told me.

Why would folk send me flowers? I better get used to this. I was temporarily a celebrity. But at this time I wanted a low profile. It was time to rest, reflect, and rejuvenate. It would take time.

The boys came home from school. Yet it stayed so quiet, everyone tiptoeing around me. The change in nuances of the light entering the living room from the ceiling windows was something I had not noticed before. It reminded me of light from another source not too long ago.

I could feel my body stretched out on the sofa, all my muscles achy, doughy, and soft. I believed I slept even when my eyes were open. Visitors started to come. My sister-in-law had me go to the bedroom and thus I avoided having to indulge in tiring chatter and regurgitating previous events again and again.

One thought that came to me was that no one asked what it felt like to be comatose. Did I know I was unconscious? Did I dream? Did I know what was happening to me? That would have opened the floodgates to my core, and I'd have blurted out what I had just visualized. Yes, no one yet knew what I had envisioned; even Doreen was still in the dark. I still did not know what to make of my vision; it was too real to be ignored. It was more than a dream; it was what had brought me out of the coma. Was it then a mere vision or something else? That evening Marlu again, over my protests, would insist I eat. The quantity was not much, but I had to sustain myself. Bedtime was so welcoming, even as I thought this was exactly where it started about two weeks ago. My arms would not wrap around my wife as we lay down, spooning her as is our nightly custom. I felt chilled under the blanket holding my wife tighter, feeling the warmth of her body nourishing me. The fan rushed cool air over us. This would have been so comfortable a few days earlier, yet it felt so more enjoyable because it might be fleeting. Maybe I would not make it through the night. I was comforted by knowing that I could actually be there to relive one of our fundamental moments in our marriage yet again, as we had for many years before.

Sleep was intermittent because I did not want to close my eyes. There were monsters out there, and I knew they were looking at me. Doreen sensed some discomfort and slid against me more, and the tears started. There were so many emotions, I was alive, I almost died (maybe I was dead and this was a dream). This was where it started. would I make it through the night? I sobbed, quietly, moistening my pillow. I was held tighter, no words were spoken. My wife knew I was a complex individual and she didn't know what to say. But she reassured me I was home and well. I needed my rest, snuggling even deeper, and I slept. The old mattress and blanket finally enveloped me with my wife. This is how a baby sleeps, I thought, smiling. Wish I could be one again. A few times, I awoke thinking I was back at the hospital. But I regained my bearings and drifted into slumber again.

It was late when I finally awoke. The boys were at school. The house was unobtrusive and soothing like a weekend when the boys were younger and actually slept in late occasionally, making it feel heavenly. Instant coffee never tasted so good. I was never one to have breakfast, yet when a bowl of cream of wheat was put into my hands I knew I had to eat. There was much lost ground to make up, plus I had no choice. I performed in slow motion; every action needed a willful coordination. Again, I felt like a child taking its first steps. But even as I succeeded in doing small tasks, recovery to do a normal day's functions was monumental. It felt like a huge granite escarpment to climb.

I was in really bad shape. My heart wasn't able to put out the blood needed to invigorate me, and if it didn't recover, this was going to be my state for the foreseeable future. Sometimes the heart recovers some of its strength and functions in a more normal capacity. This gives a patient confidence and esteem. I had neither of those now.

Again friends called and by prior arrangement, I was always asleep or occupied elsewhere. Really, talking to people who just want to jabber away was not my cup of tea at the moment. If anyone was concerned, there would be a lot of time to show it in many ways. Now I wanted peace of mind and rest. There was a beehive of emotions in my cranium trying to come out. It was a standoff for now. They were held at bay, but just barely. Left alone the buzzing would get louder, only preoccupation kept me sane. The recovery battle would come, it would be a drawn-out, bloody, wounding affair. But who exactly was the opponent, myself?, I had been bathed in the waters of Babylon not too long ago, thus all was well, and there was no need to worry. I was the chosen one. After all hadn't I survived a massive crippling heart attack, bleeding ulcer, shock liver, irritated brain, collapsed lung and respiratory failure? My vital signs could not have sustained me, even with all the meds; I was on the cusp of survival. Perhaps Stephen Hawking would call my event a singularity with myself on the event horizon. Thirty percent of people experiencing their first heart attack never have another, it is that fatal. I had survived that and much more. Surely all was forgiven. I had to have received divine blessings in my journey. Everything was going to be all right. I was special. I had seen another side to existence or a world parallel to our own. I felt it was a special honor given to me. But to show me what? What had my vision to do with surviving not in the wilderness but in our Americanized culture, which was worse than the Amazon. The hive was swarming, I had to calm myself.

"Doreen, can I have a bath?"

"Yes."

"You have to be with me," I said.

My sister-in-law looked at me severely.

"I'm too scared to have a shower myself. I can't be alone."

Understanding dawned. The maternal instinct took over. It was so refreshing again to be bathed with moisturizing soap and shampoo. The fragrances of a woman's toiletry were perfect to permeate my senses. All that feminine stuff that filled up the bathroom ledge looked scrumptious, but alas the feelings were strictly platonic.

Shortly my wife's clothes were wet as she held me up. All the steam from the shower had weakened me. I was gasping for air, my lungs were moving like bellows. Yes open the windows, set me down on the ledge, get the fan but don't leave me. I was a miserable but clean wretch, gasping soaking wet, shivering. Oh that fluffy towel felt so good. It was too heavy for me to lift let alone to use. Toweled dry in clean pajamas, a hot cup of Indian tea with milk and sugar and a few cloves and nutmeg (forget this chai fad), brewed the way it's done in the old country, refreshed me. With every swallow I felt my stomach adjust to the food presented to it. I had lost twenty pounds in the hospital; my weight was 140.

I was discovering flavors all over again, and I wanted to savor every morsel. I wanted to nap, but I was presented with a small bite again. This time it was lentil curry over white rice with a slice of Indian green mango pickle, 5 spoon full sustained me, a lick on the pickle was sufficient to send me into ecstasy. I begged to lay down and snuggle against my wife for some afternoon delight. (It was only eleven thirty a.m., but who cares.) No, I just meant sleep. After the usual clucking sounds I was allowed to pass out again. I felt so clean, my skin tingled, and my head wasn't buzzing. I was at peace for the moment.

All that I've said so far would sound appropriate for a story from a baby book. I was regressing and enjoying every moment of the experience.

It is strange when we are *in extremis*; material items don't matter. It is the basics of life that we crave. What exactly is that? Look at a baby lying contented after a feeding; it is at peace. Its lips may be suckling an imaginary object or not; its limbs are lifeless; it hears its mothers voice and may turn its head to hear the sound. A full belly, smelling of baby powder, soft garments, moisturized skin, the comfortable sounds of its mothers activities, and her smell—that is all that a baby needs to be contented. Is anyone with unlimited possessions, wealth, power, or seniority more content than that little baby? Don't we as adults feel peaceful being in the presence of that child? We get more delight holding onto a little bundle of joy than holding our most treasured expensive possession.

I knew I was regressing, but I was not embarrassed to do so. Life is simpler as an infant. There is no such thing as worry in an infant's vocabulary, except when the next breast feeding is a minute too late.

5

THE SYMPATHY CARD

In the afternoon the doorbell rang. It was another huge bouquet of flowers but addressed to Doreen. The card read:

Dear Mrs. Castellino we are very sorry that your husband has passed on. He took care of me and my family well. Please accept our condolences. He will be dearly missed.

Doreen became stiff. She didn't show me the card, but left it with the flowers. Something was amiss. Eventually that evening she showed me the card. We wondered what it meant. It came from a close family friend. Not to get upset as again and again I was told I had passed on or was at deaths door. It just brought the point home to me how close I came. Was it a practical joke, cruel and unusual in its severity?. Nope, just reality.

A few friends came and went. I was allowed to visit for a few minutes, then told I needed my rest, I preferred it that way. Visitors overstay. Their conversation stunted, grasping for words. The unnecessary chatter was taxing. But how does one pay a visit to a dear friend who has recovered from a challenging a medical crisis? We all want to show our sympathy, but do we know how? Yet there is relief at the receiving end because it's also unknown how to accept sympathy well. It is not the acute moment I talk about, but when illness or complications continue, then it is difficult to find a way to express one's sympathy. We all get fatigued, and life has to move on for the living. We cannot stop our lives to mourn for another. That evening I saw the card again, even while a close friend who I felt comfortable with visited. I showed it to him. He was not surprised as I thought he might be.

"Conrad, you were very sick," my friend said. "We all heard what was happening to you. You were the talk of the town these last few days. The medical community did not think you were going to make it. People were saying that you were in a coma at the hospital, and it does not look like you are going to make it. There was talk that you had a massive stroke and were in a vegetative state, there was talk that you were going to need a heart transplant to survive. There were just so many things going wrong with you. Every day there seemed a be a new complication."

In such situations, even a slight exaggeration passed on from person to person makes it seem that the unthinkable had happened.

"How does everyone know?" I asked.

"Conrad, everyone is talking about you. Even patients of mine are asking about you, and they don't see you. You were critically sick in the hospital. To me it is a miracle I am talking to you today. "

Such a straightforward answer was what I needed. It explained a lot.

"How does everyone know so much?" I wasn't in the least bit offended, but being the center of this kind of attention, I felt I needed to learn more.

"Computer screens were left open on purpose with your medical history on display, so with a wink it was understood where to get information from. There was incredulity when I saw some of the excerpts of your E.R. visit"

Even in the few days that I was home, many calls came in to my office from patients asking if they should send their records elsewhere, or if I would ever return to work. Some asked if I was going to be in a coma for the rest of my life. All this while I was discharged and recuperating at home!. Yes, word travels fast, but well-meant untruths travel even faster. How everyone could have known what had happened so fast? It seemed an hour-by-hour bulletin was put out on me. There was even a pharmacist who told a few patients that their prescriptions would have to be signed by another doctor because I had passed away and my practice was closing. A patient told this to one of my staff.

Of course, then I was not immediately aware of all these communications. Rather my wife, my sister-in-law, and my office staff were extremely protective of me and kept me from all these ugly rumors. I thought I saw glimpses of stress in my Doreen's face when these call came in from the office, she brushed it off as a minor business matter.

"You just rest; we can handle these nuisances."

As word had traveled, each telling of the story added some embellishment, not that mine needed much. But from the medical community, to patients, to well-wishers, and to anyone else, I was a sensation for a time.

My friend took his time explaining all this to me, as much as he dared. Every once in a while he would study my response, gauging my reaction. I had some knowledge, and what I heard filled in the gaps. I had a more rounded picture of hospitalization. There was a certain clarity in my thoughts. Medical questions beyond our discussion were clarified.

I rested that evening, digesting the day's events. This much was clear: my practice was at risk. One more bee in my scalp, but this was a big one. How the family survived, under what conditions, and where would we live in the future all hinged on coping with this one. Other people were counting on me for their livelihood as well.

And yet the competency of my sister-in-law kept me from becoming too preoccupied with my problems.

"Conrad, what would you like to eat tonight?"

"Marlu, I'm not really hungry."

"All right."

Forty-five minutes later, there was dinner.

"Prawn pulao with raita. Just a child's bowl, and eat it all up."

"But I'm not hungry."

"Of course, you're not hungry. Now, why don't you start eating?"

This was not fair, but the lady was not given to discourse. I gave up and started to eat. My attempt was feeble, and my wife was dispatched to feed me. Now that was a treat. I had to eat. Not that after a bite I didn't start to salivate, suddenly the food tasted wonderful, and I consumed it slowly. Not much was needed to fill me up, though. These incidents were like islands of respite and refuge from my upcoming maelstrom. The clouds on the horizon were distant, but grayer than yesterday and a tad closer. I could sense them.

Before bed that night I looked at my frame in the mirror. It was lean, the face was harrowed, there were scars all over, and my muscles were frail and weak. Proverbially there were dark circles around the eyes ,my face was gaunt, snug T shirts now hung loosely on my body, boxers had to be held up. The ulcer in my mouth screamed for relief.

"God, you sob. I'm done. Do what you want. I can't fight you. I don't know what you want of me. Get it over with. Tonight would be good. Please don't take it out on the family. The boys are too young. Stupid as I am they need me, young rambunctious teens. They need a male figure. My wife is ill equipped to handle such a calamity. Tell me what you want."

My reflection looked back at me with gaunt eyes, saying nothing, not even a sign.

I had a shower again, brief as it was my wife said my body was decomposing and needed freshening up. Ah, it felt so good once again. It's surprising what insignificant things and mundane activities become important when conditions change.

I would fall asleep by nine p.m., cuddled into my wife. I was freezing, she was in menopause, yet I slept well. Nestled against my wife a song from *Jesus Christ Superstar* came to mind: "Mary's Song."

Sleep and I shall soothe you

calm you and anoint you

leave all your problems behind.

Don't you know everything's alright

everything's fine

and we want you to sleep well tonight

let the world turn without you tonight

close your eyes, close your eyes

and think of nothing tonight.

The next day was the first weekend home. Family and friends were allowed to visit. I was ordered to lie on the couch. Don't move. Do need a pillow for your feet?

"Can I put my music on?" I asked feebly, in my own house. No reply, then, okay.

I played *Jesus Christ Superstar*, a super hit from the 1970s. It was everything I needed: there was heavy organ music to resonate in my depths, there was a story that I could identify with, and the complexity of the music was just like my thoughts and distracted me from myself. When I was a young lad, my brother had brought this album from a trip overseas. After one listen I had to have it. It was one of my favorite albums for many years to come.

I was looking forward to some company, I so wanted to talk about my experience. I had thought about it too much to let go. There was much greeting when the company arrived. My family was surprised to see me up, awake, and talking.

"We thought you were bed-bound." "Don't you need to rest?" "Now just sit down and do nothing." "It is so good to see you looking so good."

"We were sure you'd be exhausted and in bed."

There was much to celebrate. But no one was particularly interested in my coma, or in my thoughts. Discussion turned to what I needed to do to avoid another calamity like this. My life was dissected, much to my chagrin, and these were the changes I should make. Great discussions were held over the most meritorious foods for me—fish oil, flaxseed oil, oats, cream of wheat, less this and more that. No one was interested in hearing of the nonphysical side to the story. That was more important to me only. I could not understand it. But sensing that this was for my benefit, I silently stayed mum.

I was bursting with things to say. Please let me finish or even start, but I was so frail that my voice carried no force and thus was overruled.

Some of my family had read up on heart attacks in great depth, and I was engaged in a discussion of what precisely happened inside my heart. They were ecstatic at how much they knew, I was exhausted talking about a theme that was causing me sorrow. I was acutely aware of what had happened down to the last sticky platelet, but now was not the time, please. Let's take a rest. My mind does not want to regurgitate what happened; it wants company with solace, it wants understanding, it wants to be understood even loved now more than ever unconditionally.

Yet family and friends always talk about the latest health guru. No one has ever spoken about the mind after going through a near fatal experience. New dimensions are opened that even the patient may not comprehend, that may leave him even more vulnerable than the physical and medical aspects. He is not interested in his body as much as realizing his mind has been messed with, altered, fingered. Life may become existential. One may see that life is but one form of existence. There are other planes of existence, some of which are more appealing than the present one. Is this heaven, or the waiting parlor, or a figment of illusion so severe that we confuse it with being another plane of reality? This is cruel to say but perhaps if I was a single man with nothing to live for, the choice would be obvious. I knew that in the real world, real changes had to be made. But without comprehension of the metaphysical, the individual may be stuck by so many thoughts that he becomes incapable of making rational thought processes. His body does not matter. He has to find harmony in his physical and spiritual worlds.

The two initially seemed mutually exclusive to me. (For example, if a monk meditated for twelve hours a day, does he develop his body, his stamina, and vice versa? This is an exaggeration to show a point.) But three years later it was becoming very clear that you can be spiritual and sweaty, that nourishing one helps the other, that you can strengthen your body through visualization of physical challenges and mentally getting ready for them. We will talk more of this later.

So yes, so and so, thank you for the advice. Absolutely I should make these changes, but maybe I don't care right now. I want to understand why this happened to me. Why was I the chosen one? What was special about me? I'm worse than some people and better than others. So why was I picked on? Is there a message for me? This was a crucial question, but one of many with which I struggled and eventually came to terms with in some manner. This all disturbed me for a long time. Once I found an answer that I could maybe understand, I could earnestly start to move forward.

Although the understanding didn't happen soon, it kept me busy while I exercised, and as it was associated with pleasant activities I could rationalize better and help myself to make small tiny improvements. So even as events happened that I didn't like in some way, they were preparing me for the dialogue that was forthcoming with somebody.

It was good to see all my siblings, nephews, and nieces having my interest at heart. The youngest niece, Ava, three years old, seemed closest to me. I studied her behavior and her petulance, and whatever children do, it made sense. She was not fettered with customs, rites of behavior, a sense of right and wrong but did what she wanted. Yes, she had come from the place I had visited. Her eyes sparkled with the waters I had so recently swum in. As the day progressed, even I, a physician, did not know there were so many items good for the heart. Now if only I could consume all of them.

By evening I was wiped out. My mind was awake thinking of the days events, all the instructions and advice—diet, exercise, don't stress, do this, don't do that. These were so irrelevant to me now. But I listened. That evening I started to take measure of myself, my worth, resources, finances and other assets hidden under the mattress. My wife was not yet privy to my thoughts, or perhaps she kept her fears to herself. As we later spoke with Doreen's sister, she sensed my discomfiture.

"Conrad, you're a strong fellow. I know how much you have gone through. Just rest, take it easy for now. You'll come back, but give it time. I can see that you're not yourself, but rest for now". Said in the old country style her words were well grounded, no fancy words or eloquence, just heart felt recognition, and a profound understanding of my situation with no judgment.

And she held my vision. Yes, she knew what I was going through. Here was a simple lady, but her words were elegant, true, and deep and meaningful.

Every night was heavenly. Snuggling beside my wife kept my sanity in check and let me transition into the land of Hades. Sleep was comfortable. There was the thought that I might not make it through the night, and this was to be recurring theme that every night might be my last. I never mentioned this aloud yet was relieved to awake each morning.

The next morning being a Sunday, visitors came, hand delivered flowers, candy, flowers, huge get well cards. People I had not seen for a while even remembered me. My staff came to visit. Many clients had asked for their physician. Word now was that I had a stroke and was in a coma for good. We briefly strategized. Anyone who asked for transfers was told that I had been incapacitated for a short time but would return to work next week.

And then a wonderful lady, Ms. Jordan, a family nurse practitioner, got in touch with my office and volunteered her services for some time. This was immense. I had a little breathing room. I'm still not sure how this angel appeared, but she was welcome. Unbelievable, in return for this gesture, whenever my colleagues are indisposed I offer my services as limited as they are.

6

TAKING INVENTORY

The next day I got together with Doreen to discuss our bills and our expenses. Where were our assets? Oh no, they were tied up in the real estate market. Let me give some background: My neck of the woods was one of Americas fastest-growing boom towns. Housing prices were rising astronomically, and it was utter stupidity not to invest in real estate. A new university was being built. Other businesses were planning to move into town. Retire by age fifty-five, easily. I was launching into a new field that my wife might operate and ease into a life not regimented my medicine. I might actually have a life after all. Things were looking up.

I had practiced medicine; it was the only thing I knew, and it had served me well. Like so many other physicians it was the only life I had known and like so many others had forgotten how to live a rounded and diverse lifestyle. My whole life had been consumed by it. My free time was spent with colleagues talking about ,medicine!, no surprise there. But I was trapped by its allure and didn't know I had being sucked in, hook ,line and sinker. However, like so many financial trends with the stock market and now the real estate market, it was foolish not to invest. It was infallible, good as gold in a safe deposit box. But I found myself with properties that were once worth fortunes but now had crumbled into pennies on the dollar.

They were impossible to sell, and supporting them in my present situation was impossible. That which such a short while ago were jewels were now nothing but paste and a huge drain on my resources. Things could not continue so precariously for much longer. I would surely kill myself trying to keep up with expenses. It was not even an option. I searched my mind in vain for the miracle solution to bail myself out. Being creative, I thought something would come to mind. Try as I would there was no miracle out there. I kept to myself and, tried to live in the present day to day.

My receptionist Letty [who had helped taking the boys to school and bringing them to the hospital] called to tell my wife more people had expressed their sympathies.

"How should I reply?" she asked.

"State the truth. Doc been through a heart attack and will be returning to work. He was seriously ill for some time but has recovered. He is resting at home. And rumors of his death are not true. If they wanted I could be called at home."

I summarized things for myself. I had coverage at work, so at least one headache was held in check for now. My finances were terrible, and I would need to speak to my accountant about options. I needed to enroll in cardiac rehab (a series of activities that strengthen the body and heart and give the client confidence to become more independent) if I was going to beat this. I had a visit with my local cardiologist, he would let me know what I could and could not do and set the some guidelines to adhere to.

Doreen was doing well. No doubt her sister was taking a load off her. The boys were quiet but otherwise unchanged, which was something to monitor. Family and friends continued to offer reassurances and support.

And so the day came to a close. Fed, burped, washed, and clothed, the night was so inviting. I could be awake and not get distracted by extraneous thoughts. Even preparing for bed left me breathing hard and tired. My wife's breathing as her torso rose and fell made me slow my rate down, and thus I slumbered. I was at peace for the moment. Never did I hear "I'm having a hot flash" or "I need room."

It was when I returned to my vision and questioning the reason I had gone through such an ordeal that tumultuous thoughts raced through me. Was there a message I needed to hear? But I was at peace, I hummed "Mary's Song" ("everything's all right, everything's fine and we want you to sleep well tonight...") until sleep overtook me.

Morning came and again it was bittersweet. I was always relieved to be alive, yet the challenges of the day and the days ahead came back like mosquitoes in my brain. We had discussed all of this, yet it persisted going round and round, accomplishing nothing, frustrating me, driving peaceful thought away, fatiguing and irritating. This was still within the first week since my hospitalization. Peace, rest, no worries, were supposed to be dictum, yet those were the last thoughts on my mind. And what was this doing to my healing heart? Cortisol and other stress hormones were being churned out by my internal glands. The effect was that my blood was getting sticky and no doubt some of the work done on me was being reversed. Blood and its products would probably be sticking to the rough surfaces of my damaged heart. Just something else to worry about. I had to de-stress but did not know how and was too helpless to ask.

I had to find a distraction; otherwise I would go stir crazy. There were too many negatives. Start finding some positives or stay busy, but don't stagnate. The demons in the mind could get out of control and destroy any chances of recovery for good.

THE HOBBIES

Sitting on the deck having coffee that morning, it was a good day to start on a positive note. My youngest had a drum set, the heads almost warped, and the drumsticks looked like a rat had chewed on them. Having played in the school band back home and having a hobby of 5.1 surround sound music in high fidelity, I would combine the two. I had some knowledge of music studies, just barely, but to play the drums, only enthusiasm was needed. Playing some dance hits, I started to bang away at the drum heads. These drum sticks sure could be heavy. And why did the music have to go so fast? I barely kept up. The Beach Boys had me in mind when they wrote "Surfin' USA." It was pure fun banging away at those skins. The "crowd adulation" was welcomed. Alas, my hands got heavy, my legs trembled, and my coordination was worse than a drunk's. Four songs and I was exhausted, breathing hard, and ready for a nap.

Every venture showed how depleted my body was. There was absolutely no room to give. Just daily living activities were taxing my body to the limit. That evening I looked into the mirror again.

"I'm done, I want out. The odds are against me. I don't wanna play."

No one replied even as I waited and pondered the wretch in the mirror. He looked as if he had aged ten years in the last week or so and didn't look like he would last much longer. Tears ran and secretions clogged his nasal passages.

"End it," I moaned. "I'm done, I quit".

As the sobs wracked me in my noisy solitude, the battle would go on. I had to play but not by choice.

A walk in the front yard holding hands was exhilarating. Finally some outdoor activity. Perseverance, take it easy, pace yourself, maybe you're still alive for a reason. Give it a chance, slow down bud.

I prepared to play the skins again some more, a glutton for punishment. The band Foreigner satisfied me this time. My son closed the door on the music, I was that bad. Again exhaustion set in quick, and I took the opportunity to note my baseline condition. From here I would crawl forward.

My sleep that night was that of the warrior. I had done much, my body ached. I breathed heavy but noted no chest discomfort, something to be thankful for. And I hummed "The Lion Sleeps Tonight": "In the jungle, the quiet jungle, the lion sleeps tonight" and those strange tribal rhythms. A restful night to come, yes, drift off.

My vision came to me. "Take me back," I pleaded. It quietly nourished me, my limbs felt light, and I slept, dreamlessly till the morn.

7

THE CAR ACCIDENT: A SECOND CHANCE AT LIFE

The time was coming close when my sister-in-law would have to go home. She had spent valuable time with me and supported her sister admirably. During the crucial time when I needed focused help, she was there. News of the family here and there kept us occupied. The idle chatter was pleasantly distracting as I slumbered on my couch. That evening my wife had to drop some documents off at a friend's house.

"I'll be back soon, no more than twenty minutes." She drove off in the Prius. Time passed. Half an hour, an hour, came and went. We commented that Doreen was late. Perhaps she met someone at work. Still another hour passed. Several times we called her cell, but it went to voice mail. Panic set in. What could have happened? Was she kidnapped, in an accident, lying in an ER? Perhaps she had a heart attack somewhere.

Finally the sun had set. My chest was getting tight, my breathing slightly ragged, and my heart skipped an occasional beat. There was an adrenaline surge, which could be deadly in my situation. Some anxiolytics prescribed on my hospital discharge came in handy. Even as I tried, the possible outcomes grew only worse, and then car lights lit up the kitchen window. Someone had pulled up. Doreen and Letty had pulled up in another car. Sobbing, she walked towards us. I sensed what she thought, her concern for me could not let her speak. Good Lord, I was going to be re hospitalized soon if I didn't know what had happened. Then Doreen spoke. Less than three miles from the house, a girl had merged onto a busy street with a cell phone to her ear. She merged right into the Prius. Both cars were totaled. No one needed hospitalization, but my wife complained about a sore neck.

Why were they so late? I wondered. Letty explained that Doreen had sat on the pavement sobbing. She did not know how tell me what had happened what had happened and more importantly what effect it would have on me . Finally a police officer made her call someone to take her home. Doreen was as close to hysteria as possible. She was sobbing quietly. Concern for me was paramount in her thoughts. Would I have another heart attack? Would I need to be taken to the hospital again? Would I get angina?

My chest was tightening, but there was a different quality to the discomfort. I paused in my thoughts to understand what was happening to me. If the discomfort worsened it would mean I was in deep trouble again. Waves of apprehension rolled over me, moisture broke out on my forehead, underarms, and torso. The discomfort stayed the same. Soon the voices became faint, their outlines fuzzy, my legs turned wobbly even as someone's arms wrapped around me and gently propelled me towards the couch and letting me lean on them. There were people around me, and a cool compress was placed on my forehead, someone was sobbing quietly. A hand slipped into mine and squeezed. There were whispers of calling an ambulance. No, I wasn't going through that crap again. And squeezing back the hand I said, "No, let me rest."

Slowly with sips of iced water, rubbing of my forehead, and gentle ministrations, my near fainting spell eased. Yet I was limp as a noodle. My body had no tone or strength.

My sister-in-law asked, "Do you need anything? Should we call someone?"

Slowly with eyes closed I asked for a medicine for anxiety. Promptly something was placed in my mouth with more water. Laying back I maintained pressure with my hand.

"Not yet, just cover me. Let me lay awhile."

I rested with eyes closed but was able to pay some attention to what was happening around me. Muted voices sounded concerned. There were too many people counting on me. I had to rally back. The chest discomfort had not worsened and was perhaps a tad less constricting. Slowly I willed my eyes open, forcing myself to stay under control. Squeezing my wife's hand some more, letting her know I was coming around.

"I'm getting better. No ambulance."

I maintained control barely. The feeling passed. I was lucky this time.

Through her teary eyes she studied me to see which direction I was headed. My sister-in-law also was studying my reaction. Never did I feel like hiding my emotions like just now.

"Hang on, young man," I said to myself. "Just hang on. The man upstairs is still pitching. You're still at bat. The crowd is waiting for the clutch play."

I would no, could not give in, I would at least hold my own.

I tried to speak, but a cotton mouth jumbled my words. I had to stay down. Too many people would be affected if I broke down. It is strange that even as the captain, I was the weakest member of the team. But I had to be an example to others right now. Slowly I righted my thoughts. I would survive this spell and bat again.

Doreen slowly filled us in on the details of the accident, the most vital being that no was hurt or hospitalized.

"Doreen, yes, no one is hurt, we can take care of the car later. We are not done yet, it will be fine. I am surviving again. We are still alive, and we will be okay."

Holding onto me muffled her sobs. We came around.

"I will live through this and more," I mumbled to the SOB upstairs. "What do you have for me next? Is that the best you can do, you miserable bastard? Are you through? Face me, you piece of crap, I'll take you on." Unmentionables flowed freely from my mouth quenching my rage and bitterness. This was shaping up to be a battle of attrition. I would go down swinging, brutal as the odds were they had just gotten worse yet I would fight on.

Unmentionables stayed buried within. I was being toyed with and helpless again to control my fate.

Doreen, again got scolded by her sister for getting into an accident. It was a touch of comic relief. I smiled as I thought back to when I dated Doreen back home. Any truancy and she would get it from her sister, and by default so would I. Twenty years later it was happening again. But the stakes were so much higher this time.

As she later told me after her sister had gone back home, Doreen got another scolding in private. This news would have killed me. Don't I have any shame? and on it went, sister to sister, and me the cause of it. Yes, life is devious and delicious, I relished the story. Humanity was present still in the world. I was going to weather this just fine, but first let me pull this nail out of the coffin lid. I was not done yet.

The evening passed quietly. We ate dinner, which was again forced on me. But in spite of my denials I knew I needed nourishment. I was the silent study of my family, though Doreen was the one in pain.

A shower again; My muscles had knotted up, and there was a ferocious ache at the base of my neck. Today after the rituals of the day were done, I lay on Doreen's lap as the sisters spoke and prattled about this and that. Glimpses came to me when I recognized a name in the conversation. Tensions were easing, mostly I was staying control.

That night was a different matter. The mood somber, Doreen lay in my arms, sniffling, clearing her passages, she was choked up.

"We can't take much more of this. Are you mad at me? Will you be alright?"

Her tears flowed. Deep sobs and convulsions shook us on the bed. I felt helpless, targeted, and defenseless. Can we take any more? Yes, we had to.

Somehow I felt it was not my end, otherwise I would have been done with by now. Here was an epic struggle, the outcome already known to me: I would survive, but like a *Mad Max* movie, the story takes many twists and turns until the very end.

Jesus Christ Superstar again played in the background, and we slowly got in control of our emotions, or maybe we were just plain exhausted. The pillows were wet, stained with our tears waiting for news of the next calamity to overtake us. I hummed the lyrics in my head as we quieted down:

Listen Jesus I don't like what I see

All I ask is that you listen to me

We are occupied

Have you forgotten how put down we are?

I am frightened by the crowd

We are getting much too loud

It was beautiful, but now it's gone sour

Yes it' s all gone sour,---

Sleep came soon, we were too tired to stay awake, and everything was well in spite of the new challenge. Restlessness disturbed my wife, the neck was stiffening up. Sleep was fragmented, but it did come bringing the morn on us again. That day the sisters went shopping. Soon she would leave to go home, and a few novelties had to be purchased. Even being left alone for a short while made me nervous.

"Please keep your cell phone as close as possible," I said as they went their way.

Going to the drum set I started playing. This time I tried "We Are the Champions," by Queen. I also played some Elton John and of course Foreigner. I just enjoyed the music tried to keep beat with the foot pedal and snare whenever possible, with not much success.

I tried to fathom the significance of the previous evening's events. It did not add up to anything constructive. Was my wife also being tested? What was her folly? My conclusion was that this is part of the trial, probably one that has not ended. Surely there was more on the way, of that I was sure, but so much brutality! I knew I was strong, but give a man some breathing room. Why did I have to be tested so severely? Really the only thing that kept me going was that the boys needed me, and they would need me even more. I was going to be vital in their life, but not right now.

Soon I was in a light sweat from banging away at the skins. I was still tiring easily. I knew now that (1), more was in store, (2) I would survive, and (3) it was going to be a brutal ride to get there, wherever that was.

My physical condition had deteriorated even more in spite of all the attention. My pants were held up by a belt cinched tightly at the waist. Jeans felt too heavy. It was cool to me although the temperature outside was in the nineties.

I needed help to get my strength back. The average rest period for a person who has undergone an event like mine is about three to six months. That period is supposed to be spent in a calm, peaceful lifestyle, with light activity slowly increasing, to make sure the heart was recovering and stress free. The more stress and anxiety a person has the more rapid the heartbeat, the more likely to have complications such as angina, congestive heart failure, irregular heart rate, which is the most common cause of sudden death after a heart attack. So I was striking out on all counts, except the light activity. Rest was impossible with the bees buzzing in my head. There was plenty of stress around. Although I felt my heart wanted to take off, the meds were keeping it under control. I had to know where my meds were at all times, and so did the rest of the family in case I needed emergency help.

When my sister-in-law left, I felt another leg get wobbly under the table. She had been a pillar of strength for us at a very difficult period and had given fully of herself to help us. I needed more time to feel comfortable again. But who was I kidding? This was going to be a long, drawn out war of attrition. But it was not the body I was concerned about, it was my mind. When a processor is sparking, you know the rest of the computer is malfunctioning; fix the hard drive, and the rest falls into place.

8

AUNT MIMI

Let's roll forward a few weeks from our last encounter. As all the issues from the accident wrapped up and nothing else transpired, we began to breathe more easily. Perhaps that was a solitary event after all, coincidental. Doreen's stiff neck resolved with analgesics, warm compresses, and lots of stretching exercises. Even as an invalid I did what I did best, treat people even if they were family.

Not too far from where we lived, my brother's wife's parents lived. Aunt Mimi and Bob. When we came over to America back in the 1980s, fresh off the boat and wet behind the ears, they entertained us royally. My first Thanksgiving at their home was a wonder. I could not believe the scrumptious meal set out. No short cuts were taken. They were fine hosts to their son-in-law's family. Being a large clan it always took some consideration to invite us en mass, yet we never felt like an imposition, and I learnt a lot of local culture when I visited with them.

One day after I had come back to California following my residency on the East Coast, Bob sat down with me. We had a long talk while a party went on. Bob spoke his mind gently but with authority. He had asked about my future plans. Always gracious he invited us to visit in his new house. They had left the Bay Area to settle in a retirement community 2 hours away and close to me . We did and always enjoyed ourselves, clowning, playing the fool and getting into trouble. On a particular july 4th pool party, Randy[his son] and I tried to destroy a huge watermelon by hammering it into the swimming pool. It was rib cracking fun till Aunt Mimi demolished us with a severe scolding that still leaves my ears ringing.

"Conrad, you'll have been in America less than ten years and you'll have done tremendously for yourself. You'll have paid your dues and then some. Now you come along and are starting out on the right foot, you and your brothers have got it together. So many of us Americans can't compare."

And so it went on. I always appreciated talking with Bob. He spoke straight from the heart. Was mild mannered and always was supportive toward us.

When Bob passed away a few years later, I had the pleasure of holding his hand. He remembered me when we visited in the hospital. I sat on his bed and we exchanged pleasantries.

He knew his end was near and we spoke of it openly. We spoke briefly but deeply as he would doze off unexpectedly. I was comfortable that Bob was at peace. Two days later he passed away in Oakdale with his family and us beside him.

Fast forward to the present; The boys[my son Austin and his cousin Dylan] were to meet at Aunt Mimi's on Tuesday. The next day was Austin's his birthday, and they were going to go to a place called Knights Ferry for a large breakfast, river rafting and a few days of fun-filled activity. They were to leave that evening. Austin was complaining as mom felt tired and wanted to go the next morning. I agreed, Mummy is tired, reflecting my own feelings. It is okay to leave in the morning and thus the boy accepted the change in his fate.

The next morning as I stayed at home, Doreen left for Oakdale with the boys. It was around nine a.m., and the phone rang. It was Bernie asking where Austin was.

"On his way to Oakdale."

"With whom?"

"Doreen"

"Are you sure?"

"Didn't he go last night?"

"Nope. Doreen was tired, so they left this morning."

"Are you sure?" What did I sense in his voice?

"Yes, they left half hour ago. I saw them leave"

There was puzzlement on the line, and I could sense he was not happy with the answer.

"Okay," he replied.

Shortly thereafter my sister called asking much the same question: where is Austin?

"He is with mummy headed to Oakdale."

"Are you sure?"

"Yes. I saw them leave about an hour ago."

"Does she have her cell phone?"

"Yes."

"Alright take care of yourself."

I sense an urgency to break away. I was puzzled and called Doreen to ask if everything was okay.

"Yes. We are near Oakdale. Wait hold on there is a call coming in. Let me call you back."

This was mystifying. Why was everyone interested in Austin? I knew everyone was okay, so I would not worry. Doreen would be home soon. And again the bees started buzzing furiously in my head.

Several minutes later Doreen called back. She would be leaving for home soon.

"Is everything okay? Everyone is calling for Austin."

"Oh, yes, everyone one is fine. They are just planning a surprise for him. I'll see you soon."

When they pulled up to the house, Austin got out of the car!. Was he not supposed to be elsewhere?

"Let's go in. I need you to prepare yourself."

Dampness permeated my clothes, and my mouth became dry. There was dead silence all around. My head felt light, my vision became tunneled, my limbs heavy, and a vice gripped my chest gently yet firmly. Good Lord, what is this all about?

As I sat down the boys stayed distracted yet silent. Doreen was not sure what to say. I knew this was for my benefit but I had to know and soon. Either way I was in agony.

Slowly, haltingly Doreen said there had been an accident in Oakdale this morning about an hour ago. Aunt Mimi and Dylan were in a car accident. They were T-boned on the freeway. Aunt Mimi passed away on the spot. Dylan is in a coma and was flown by helicopter to a trauma center.

"Why was everyone inquiring about Austin?".

"They thought he had gone last night and was in the vehicle and the emergency crew were looking for him at the accident scene. They called you, at hom e as they did not find him at the accident site".

"As bad as it was it could have been much worse, and Bernie held his thoughts and feelings in as he inquired about Austin's where abouts. "My gosh, I don't know what to say!" And for a big mouth like me that was brutally frank. My brother with tragedy of the most serious kind had called me fighting his feelings and as nonchalantly as possible was looking out for my sons well being. He had done well, I had no idea anything bad had transpired"

"How is Dylan doing?"

"They don't know how serious he is or what injuries he has. Bernie and his wife are going there now, a drive of a couple of hours."

Absolutely asinine. How could this happen? Yet that was not important. There were so many unspoken words, so many thoughts left hanging on a thread. There was nothing to say but much to be sad for. For once the world was not ego-centric. I could feel the suffering my brother and his family were enduring, their anguish just a breath away. I wished no accident would befall them as they drove to the hospital as so likely to happen, finding out some more detail. The irony was cruel. Yet I felt for my brother, who called me and stayed calm while trying to find out about my son.

I went into the bedroom, Doreen in tow. I buried my head on her lap and sobbed away for eternity. There was so much pain around me, it was pervasive. I fell into its clutches, and valued my life and survival like never before. Today I was lucky in so many ways.

A few more calls came in to ask about Austin again during the day. We were quiet. The buzzing faded into the background. What more was in store for the family?

Later in talking to Austin, in his own way knew Dylan would be fine, and that was that. As long as he looked comfortable, I was alright prying. The phone lines stayed busy the whole evening. I kept to myself. That night, holding each other, words were not necessary. Just the most confounding event that could ever have happened.

As we began to drop off into sleep, I saw Aunt Mimi on the other side. She was comfortable but confused as to where she was. Searching for bearings there were none, but I saw no anxiety or agitation. I wished I could have reached her, but alas that connection was illusory.

The next morning my wife aroused me to say that Dylan was awake and seemed good, but the doctors would not let him move. They were still checking him out. The family wanted to visit, yet the distance was far and there too much anxiety. Another accident was what I was thinking. We were all too emotional to make driving safe.

Soon my nephew was released from the hospital. Mimi's funeral was held that weekend. I chose not to attend. Emotionally I could not face anyone in a fate that until so recently was going to be mine. With every hour that passed I couldn't but think I was reliving my recent past again. This incident was too close to me. The suffering that my brother and his family were feeling was palpable. It surrounded me like a miasma that was unshakable. I was reliving my near miss again. Thus I asked my brother permission not to attend. My family did go for the memorial services, Austin being close to his cousin.

I kept busy trying to play on the drums that day, yet I could see Aunt Mimi trying to find her way on the other side. Tears streamed down my face as I willed her to find meaning in her new surroundings. The pain of death that was so close to me was now on someone I knew so well. Did I feel guilt that I was spared? No, I still believed that there was a reason for my survival. Death would have spared me so much of the pain I had felt and was going to feel for several years to come.

I could not wait for the family to come home. Solitude was not becoming me and was even terrifying. Aunt Mimi was laid to rest beside Bob. Her wake was attended by so many people who had known her and her family, and many of us from overseas who had incorporated Aunt Mimi into our own culture were there to grieve as well.

For three years after my heart attack, I was unable to attend a funeral. It was too close to home.

9

RECOVERY 101

As the days agonizingly passed, so did a smorgasbord of emotions pass through me. These feelings were precipitated by calls from my staff saying that some clients believed I'd had a stroke and would not return to work, or that I had passed away. So I decided to return to work. It was a confounding decision, stay at home and let the bad news flow on, making me more nervous, or bite the bullet go against convention, return to work, keep myself occupied and hang on. The latter seemed preferable as doing nothing was aggravating me while my world continued to crumble around me.

It was not something I wished to do but there were so many compelling factors, some of them unrealistic that forced the decision on me. In a perfect setting, I would have awakened at ten in the morning most days, been waited on hand and foot for a month or more, provided with delicacies to tantalize me, had a light workout, make phone calls to old friends, slowly resolve some family and business matters not work related, take long afternoon siestas, and socialized some in the evening. I'd do other non-stress activities. But this illusion had to be laid asunder. I had to stick to my plan if we were going to make it and survive in any meaningful way.

On my first day, Doreen drove me to the office. It seemed alien to me, and a mild panic attack set in. There were butterflies in my stomach. What impression was I giving with my pale thin frame?

My fears were immediately put to rest by my first few social encounters.

"Doc, it is so good to see you."

"Heard you were awful sick, glad to see you back."

If people had any reservations, they hid them well. Thus reassured that I was not scaring anyone, the rest became much easier. My self-esteem lifted a tad. I worked for an hour at a time initially. Most of the time I was sicker than those who came to see me, but I slogged through the day. Much, many years later those patients told me I looked like a shadow of myself and didn't give me high odds of survival, yet they stuck with me.

Even an hour left me exhausted mentally and physically. As much as I needed to recuperate, it would have to wait until later. To date there was not much opportunity to grieve for myself and let the healing begin mentally. Later I learned of this feeling that one could actually grieve for oneself, and yet looking back it makes good sense. It lets the past slide by and lets the healing begin. My world had been filled with one calamity after another, without respite.

At the end of each work day I came home exhausted. I'd crash for hours and otherwise think of when I would become stronger again. Yet my presence at work had a stabilizing influence. Many who came in were surprised to see me. We visited more than anything else. And word got out in our small town that I was working again. As tiring as it was, it kept me occupied and lent structure to my day. I felt this was one situation that I could actually control. Everything else had me on a string like a puppet. I could still do my job, barely. But I was giving myself time.

I started a rehab program to strengthen myself, especially the heart. It is most remarkable how the human body disintegrates when it is immobilized or not used. Muscles waste, breathing capacity decreases, reflexes slow down, digestion weakens, the mind stagnates. Even day-to-day activities become a huge chore; taking out the garbage becomes the event of the day.

Cardiac rehab is a fantastic way to build confidence in oneself. The rehab team had worked with many patients and understood what I had gone through and what to expect as I progressed. Through the grapevine, the team knew of my calamity but they had heard I may be permanently incapacitated. They knew my limitations but were also encouraging.

The initial workouts were baby steps. Walking on a treadmill at one mile per hour; range of motion exercises with 2.5-pound weights, stationary bicycle, hand cyclometer, pulleys, and springs. My wife observed me for the first session. It was remarkable to find out how strong I was: close to zero. Yet I stayed with my instructors. Those guys and gals, sensing my insecurity, were so close to me the whole of that session I could not help but feel reassured. Monitor leads on my chest were attached to a display that gave my heart rate and other information to tell the team if it was struggling. Blood pressure was checked every few minutes and they kept their eye on you to look for any sign of distress. This was a Herculean day for me. However seeing others who had progressed through the same struggles gave me confidence. In healthy times, I could bench press 185 pounds and use 30-pound dumbbells.

I saw others around me who had suffered a fate similar to mine, but I was the youngest. I was enlightened by the friends I made. Seeing others working away gave me a boost. Surely if some of these guys had recovered so much, so could I. The team was always there to reassure me that given time, consistency, and dedication I would make a huge recovery. However the final outcome would depend on how well my heart recovered some of its lost function and how much the remaining could compensate for the dead portion. This is colloquially known as remodeling of the heart. After ten minutes, we had a cookie break. It was the best break I had ever had.

At the end of my first session everything looked good. I was elated yet humbled. No doubt the workout had released endorphins in my body giving me a sense of well-being. I went home to a well-deserved rest. Shower, lunch, and off to bed. For all my carrying on you would have thought I had run a marathon.

"One day at a time, sweet Jesus, is all I'm asking of you. Give me the strength to live one day at a time."

I looked forward to my next outing to the rehab center. Slowly, the sessions got better, and I could actually see where I had made a minuscule improvement. Each time I went in, the speed on the treadmill increased in one-tenth increments and the duration by a minute. Yet seeing the numbers go up gave me confidence that I could get better. This was rewarding, positive strokes; I had not felt good about anything for so long. This was fantastic. My doom and gloom lightened up one notch. There might be hope after all. This was something I was in control of, and there were no surprises, only positive reinforcement. Initially my heart rate would accelerate quickly, but as I stayed with it the rate would slow down to where it should be for the level of activity. There was no irregular rate, very reassuring, and my blood pressure stayed steady. A light sweat would cool me at the end. This was living. Food tasted good, a slight appetite developed, and sleep was more restful. There were periods of sunshine piercing the clouds every now and then.

I visualized what was happening in my heart. Those blood vessels that were so badly obstructed and then manipulated were scarred and uneven. There was a wire-mesh stent supporting the walls and keeping them patent. There was a medicine in the stent that prevented further blockage from developing there for now. Yet the diameters of the blood vessels were narrow. Exercise would promote their dilation and increase the blood supply. Some parts that were damaged and not working would slowly start pumping again. As more blood flowed through my damaged heart and the rest of my body, I became stronger. My sense of well-being and hope grew.

I took no time for disability . None. And that was foolish. I should have been off for at least three months, yet I made work part of my rehab. The real truth was that I could not see myself at home doing nothing. There was so much on my agenda that distracting thoughts were always present. Plus there were two other factors. I could not see myself disabled. There was no point fighting if I was going to rot for the rest of my life, and that is what I equated it to. From the practical aspect we needed the income to start rebuilding ourselves and repairing the damage. This would work for me. I would make to even if it cost me my life.

There were still hurdles to overcome, but I had made a few faltering steps toward my recovery.

10

THE FINANCIAL
QUAGMIRE

Rehab continued to perk me up. I continued to strengthen as the weeks passed. Or maybe it would be better to say that at least I was not regressing. Now came the time to determine what my lifestyle was going to be for the next few years. Could I work at the frenetic pace I was used to? Did I want to or need to? Actually the question should have been what is the right balance to strike in my life?

I did not want to work as I had been; it would have been suicidal. More to the point—I could not work that way. I wanted to change the balance in my life, to become more rounded in my daily activities.

I realized that I had lived to work, but from now on work would only be a part of my life. I would try very hard from this point to develop new goals, new boundaries, and a different landscape from the one that previously filled my life. That landscape would guide me on my new path, wherever that leads me. Other activities that would occupy me were vaguely in my mind but had not crystallized yet. I had no desire to rush things along.

My second motto would be, "Take your time, don't rush." My third would be "rearrange my priorities." What was most important going forward? It could not be what had driven me before.

I had these caveats in mind: I knew my finances had to be rearranged. So far I had been studying my situation. I had to make difficult decisions to salvage what I could and not get blindsided by a future calamity, which was very possible, given my predicament.

My grief in knowing what I had to do was tremendous, yet in previous dialogues with my maker, I had cussed him out good for this additional curse (or blessing). I had looked in my mirror and spoke with the man. I heard no reply, but a vague plan of what needed to be done emerged. In my mind I had already thought of living under a bridge somewhere, and actually, after I thought it through, it didn't seem that bad of an idea. Imagine the worst, and if you can live with that, everything else seems doable. I have a wonderful friend, Clarence, a very nonchalant fellow, experienced in the ways of the world yet down to earth. I had bounced my scenario off him.

Matter-of-factly he replied: "I'll come to visit under the bridge. Make sure you have a mattress for me, and for dinner, we'll go dive in the McDonald's Dumpster.

"Conrad," he continued, "you've done a pretty fantastic job over the years. Not too many people can hold a light to you. Crap can happen to anybody. Think of what you've accomplished. Forget the small stuff."

The "small stuff" happened to be my reputation, my standing, my net worth, my stupidity. Those were hollow possessions now, of no value to me.

Thus my biggest nightmare turned into a pleasant repartee. Clarence always knew how to look at a problem with so much street wisdom. He knew how to separate the fluff and fear and put them in their proper place. I really liked him. Whenever he came to my office we would spend more time shooting the bull than doing with medicine. Always a welcome face to my mundane days. Always wit with wisdom.

I proceeded with the okay of my self-appointed guru, that this was the right thing to do, instead of killing myself with overworking again. My attorney crystallized my thoughts further and really did grunt work that saved me a lot of grief and kept me from imploding on my thoughts. I visited with another legal specialist who specialized in financial matters. I needed a good plan, because the courts cared nothing of illnesses. They looked only at numbers, and everything had to be done right.

I had a lot of assets against my name alone, but with that came a lot of debt. The debt load was going to kill me. To explain—when you borrow to buy property, you pay the interest and a part of the principal on a regular basis. I could not sustain that amount of effort any more. In better times with prices shooting through the roof, there was no need to worry. Properties could be flipped, the loan paid off, and a profit realized. But with the collapse of the economy and particularly the real estate market, I was left with properties that were losing value rapidly. Loans that had to be paid off were eating into paychecks. So I either had to work hard or get rid of the debt to give me some freedom and breathing room.

Attorneys are pretty nice people. I may not approve of the laws of the land crafted by many smart people and altered so often that you needed to be a lawyer to make sense of it all. The law in my opinion has little to do with right or wrong; rather it is a set of rules that define and redefine the legal terms in our vocabulary that seem opposite of what our interpretation of the situation might be. Thus my new acquaintances educated me about what my financial options might be. After several meetings, the best way out seemed to be to file for chapter 7 reorganization. My financial records had to be poured over to make me as needy as possible.

When my wife and I went to the courthouse, we were astounded at the number of people filing for bankruptcy. Our lawyer told us that on the average, about five hundred people were filing for some type of reorganization on a weekly basis. This seemed high. However as we visited the courts several times, there were no less than thirty people for the same reason on each occasion. The personal suffering endured by so many as the economy faltered, hit home. The government had taken care of the big corporations with our taxes, but no one helped individual citizens. No one was unduly perturbed by what was happening to the man in the street. Horrendous as the situation was, there was safety in numbers. My personal sense of failure evaporated. This was a failure of the collective consciousness of our society. We had worshipped a pagan god—greed. This was as massive as the exodus in the Bible and just as telling. The whole country seemed deeply affected, and I did not feel as bad in my predicament.

We were saved for last and asked to sit at the table and sworn in. The first session consisted of preliminaries, submitting documentation, and answering routine questions. After the judge had finished the routine stuff, I would say that the contents of our file piqued his interest. We were studied carefully up and down. I knew a mental assessment was being made. Were we up to any shenanigans? Was there unreported income or assets? We were in for special treatment.

On the next occasion we were again saved for last. This time we were asked deep probing questions. The judge seemed after some holes in our story. We were under the magnifying glass and spotlight together. Initially I had told my attorney this was unnerving.

"Could I do jail time?" I asked. It seemed more pleasant than what the judge was after.

"No," he reassured us. "If your case was not worthy of reorganization I would not have taken it, and you genuinely qualify for reorganization. It is just that the system is packed with people filing for bankruptcy. The judge has heard every story, every lie. There is no humanity in the process, but you won't go to jail."

Initially I was embarrassed about having to file. It was undignified to do such a despicable a thing. It meant personal failure and that I was not much better than a criminal or a deadbeat. Smarting from my own accusations, I kept lurching forward with great trepidation. I was a worthless bum. But seeing so many others reassured me that obviously I was not the only one. On the second visit, I was almost inarticulate from the suspense and the stern surroundings. I was ready to collapse in more ways than one. This time as we sat down and the judge perused our file, I took a chance.

"Your honor, sir, may I explain why I am filing for reorganization?"

The stern look told me I was only getting into more trouble. My lawyer put his hand on my forearm, to restrain me. I should have withered away right there, but the judge was taken aback by my question and apparently wondering what mischief I was up to. He said to proceed.

I proceeded to narrate my recent health calamity—the hospitalization, life support, inability to work as hard as I used to, as consistently as I had, and thus I could not keep up with my commitments. I was succinct and as comprehensive as possible.

We continued to be studied.

"Judge, sir, may I show you some documentation supporting my story?" "What might that be?" The guy sounded like he might be human after all.

"Sir, here is a discharge summary from my recent hospitalization." He reviewed it carefully.

"Could you tell me more? Did this really happen to you?" He looked at Doreen as he spoke to me. No doubt her expressions would support or negate me. I could sink myself for good into quicksand and never be seen again. My attorney would have wrenched my forearm off, if only it hadn't been so sweaty.

Close as I was to an apoplectic state, there was nothing to lose. I explained more, trying to keep my answers brief. If there was a gap in the conversation, I willed myself to be quiet until his honor spoke again and then only replied to his questions.

Somberly he leaned back in his chair and took his time to peruse the documentation.

"If you wish, sir, I could sign a release so that you may see my whole medical chart from the hospitalization." Touch down or out of bounds? Not that it mattered.

When he looked up, there was a really a human expression on his face. As he leaned back his posture was less formal, the iron expression softened just a little, was he a trite lost as he shuffled documents, Adams apple bobbing he searched for words.

"I believe what you have told me." His voice was soft, conversational, and almost consoling. "Yet I do have to do what the courts have appointed me to do."

"I understand, sir, I just wanted to let the court know why a person in my situation is filing for reorganization. That's all."

"Thank you."

The tone had changed; the outcome would not. Yet from that point forward he treated us more humanely. Like an executioner, he had to discharge his duties. All further queries were directed to my attorney, but the edge had gone from the judge's voice. It was more cursory but no less deadly.

As we left that second time, he wished me well and told me to take better care of myself. Outside the room I trembled as my attorney steadied me.

"That was the most unexpected move any client has ever made in this room." Half of him wanted to choke me, and the other half wanted to hug me.

"Conrad, this won't change much, but I think the going will be easier."

In all we were called back seven times, another record for my attorney on a single case. Nothing changed. We were always called last, it seemed. The legal aspect was carried out as it should have, but the judge gave me some respect and once even inquired how my recovery was coming along.

To spare myself embarrassment, let me say all the wealth and possessions I had acquired in my professional life except for a very small amount was gone. But my debt was also erased. There was respite, breathing room; the gods on Olympus having had their entertainment would let me live another day. Shylock had his pound of flesh, but it didn't turn out to be that painful. I would say that my foresight in anticipating the process and crying my heart out with the man upstairs had exhausted my emotions in this matter. I was not a criminal. My situation was extraordinary; this was not to be unexpected. I felt jubilation after everything was lost. We were square with the law. My debtors would have to wait another day. The embarrassment was gone. There was actually grudging respect for the legal system. It might be fair after all. Doreen commented that she thought I would collapse literally a few times during, yet it was I who helped steady her through the worst. Stronger now but not by much, I was pleased with myself for enduring this marathon with so little angst.

Already I was planning for the day when I would be financially viable again. My first goal was to make sure my bills would be paid and current; the second would be to have enough liquid assets in hand to last two years should another calamity befall me. This would help my wife if the family had to transition into her next situation more peacefully. There was now a reason to return to work. I could actually keep what I made. Slowly I found my stamina increasing. This was more of a mental thing. Surely with the reorganization behind me and the personal test that went with it which I had cleared life had to get better. One of the biggest hurdles was behind me. The buzzing in my head eased a bit, the ferocity decreased another notch. I could take one step back from the edge of the precipice.

I turned my attention to building my practice again. I would have more time to devote to recovery, rehab, and long-range goals that were only three months out at this time. I didn't want to look beyond such a time frame as the future was still unpredictable. Yet the mind was cleared from one very serious recurrent nightmare. So many problems were cleared at once in the courtroom, though the legalities would go on for a long time.

On a slightly more sinister note, there were other factors that held my practice down. It was by sheer coincidence that I found out, and that in itself is another long story to be written one day.

There is much that can be said about the ethics of the practice and business of medicine. If most physicians practice medicine and never see huge financial gains, it's that there are many non-physicians who impact our resources. The bill you receive from a doctor's visit or a procedure is only the tip off the iceberg. There is great misuse of everyone's personal information, including doctors' professional identity. We don't need to trim the health care budget; existing funds are more than adequate to provide good care to every American. We instead have to cut down on fraud, do less testing, spend money where it will have the most impact, and not get derailed by the newest gizmo to come along that is praised by some committee.

There is very little unbiased research conducted in the medical field. Only the most expensive and lucrative treatment alternatives are submitted to the patient. We could do so much more to help ourselves and still stay in good health by simple, inexpensive care options that patients will never learn of. Medical school, with its attendant cost of fifty thousand dollars a year for at least four years, plus four years of pre-med studies and at least three years of residency, makes doctors fodder for the health care business unwittingly. There is also an absence of teaching on the economics of medicine. Unfortunately some of us have caught on and gone over to the dark side.

The majority practice good medicine as they have been taught, but subterranean forces distort the realities and muddy the waters so insidiously that most physicians don't know how to support a system so vast that it seems woven into the practice of medicine. Thus physicians are held accountable for that about which they know little. Costs could come down, quality of care could go up, physicians would be more humane, and medical care could be tailored to patients rather than our shotgun approach of medical budget cuts. The world would be a better place. Really!

11

TALK THERAPY

The financial rearrangements made took about six months. Going to the courthouse was always stressful. I met several people there from my city. They were sometimes mortified to see me and wanted to ask why I was there, but they never did. I always opened the dialogue, letting them know I was here with the same financial reorganization issues. They were always surprised to find me in a similar predicament, but that made it easier for them to speak of what had transpired with them. The stories had a common thread: overextended financially, house loan mortgage going up, fewer hours at work leading to an income reduction, investing in second homes that they could not afford, loans on land that was now never going to be developed, a spouse laid off or wages cut. Many business owners were there. They had invested so much in the boom that when the crash came their inventory had to be financed and refinanced. But with no sales, they could not sustain extra payments.

Initially the banks would not work with clients, and the default rate on homes skyrocketed. The government plan to support individuals in need went nowhere. I saw little benefit from the aid package. Sure it was talked about a lot, but it was nowhere to be had, and no loan company was willing to give out this valuable information. I still wonder where most of those funds went. In our city with a foreclosure rate of over 10 percent, unemployment close to 20 percent, excluding those who took a big income cut, there should have been a federal loan assistance bureau so you knew the facts and knew where to go for help. As it stood one was left on their own to find the way in a very muddled scenario.

Yet there was nothing, no help no concrete directions to help one along and no matter how severe the hardship, many of the loan companies would not talk to you unless you missed a few payments.

Thus I found it therapeutic to talk about my situation, and many people wanted to engage me about how I went about it in great detail. I knew this applied to them personally, and I felt no shame in my situation. More importantly, since I was not likely to die in the near future, I looked for a message to be learned by this chapter in my life. I was beyond shame. What could I learn about myself? I was a glutton for punishment, that was for sure. But were my limits being explored?

Yet that had happened in the not too distant past. There was a lesson to be had from this experience, and thus I found that talking about my experience made it easier for others to confide in me. Others seemed to benefit from hearing my story, and I could see their own plans crystallizing. I became more of a counselor in these difficult times, and the more I told my story in all its gory details, the more it did not make seem right to me. There was something maybe not as gloomy also to be learnt. So I knew the path I had to follow to find another layer of revelation. But, oh, the price I had paid!

I came to some realization that telling others of my tribulations was of some intrinsic value. A piece of me fell back into place and somehow I worried less. Could it be that this was why I was still around? I felt good that others benefited from my telling.

12

RECOVERY 102

During my financial calamity, I kept with my cardiac rehab classes. Slowly, I progressed up the ladder of stamina, strength, and self-confidence. The pace on the treadmill increased, up to 2.2 mph. I was handling five to ten pound weights. I could last now up to five minutes on the aerobic exercises. My strength on the hand cyclometer increased. Slowly I pulled up with the laggards. The staff was so wonderful. They noted every improvement and continued to give support and encouragement. Physically I started to feel that I might make it.

The increased stamina gave me reason to exercise on my own. I had come a long way from being afraid to shower alone! Vague plans formed in my mind about how I could continue workouts on my own in a more concerted and fruitful manner.

There was a field across the road from where I lived with wonderful paths to walk on. In the evening with the sun setting behind a newly built university far in the distance, one could forget worries and think that there was peace in the world. With my wife in tow, we crossed the road, into the corn fields and slowly wandered about a hundred yards and back. Whoopee! That was good. I even forgave the occasional gnat sting. The dust reminded me of another walk I had taken recently. Tippy, my youngest son's pet, kept us company. He was ecstatic to be chasing rodents, crickets, and what else, while myself and Doreen, like tortoises, plodded along.

The path through the fields was more than physical. As I walked, I symbolically hung each of my problems on a tree. I divested myself of all worries and enjoyed a stress free activity. On the way back these problems would come nether to me. It's remarkable how, once you get used to an activity, it takes on a mind on of its own, you start to long for it, yet it takes a certain determination to push past the point from where it's a challenge to enjoyment. For several weeks it is difficult to stick to a schedule. Your muscles get sore easily, fatigue is quick to set in, and it just doesn't feel right. Keep at it, and the rhythm becomes carefree, and one does not consciously have to think of coordinating activity. It is then that the mind is at rest and wanders. Positive thoughts flood in, and at the end it has felt good to workout.

Slowly over the months I could stand about a quarter of a mile return trip. Confidence increased. I returned to the gym near my house. Slowly I worked up to ten-pound dumbbells. I could do biceps curls, bench presses, lat pull downs, military presses, squats, and triceps extensions. Pulley exercises were used to augment my free weight workouts.

As my confidence grew, so did the sessions. From twenty minutes of exercise, I was up to almost forty-five minutes, although brakes were many. I always started by walking on the treadmill for ten minutes. From there I did the weight stuff, and at the end again hit the treadmill for another ten minutes. Every step I took without any chest discomfort gave me courage to take the next step, and so on.

But I lacked consistency. It was easy to miss a couple of workouts. There was always an excuse, and then it was that much more difficult to get going again. I was always playing catch up. It is surprising how rapidly the human body gets deconditioned. To boost me along I remembered my high school physics: a body at rest stays at rest; a body in motion stays in motion. The endorphin surge always rested me afterward and made me feel lighter and less caring of my troubles. Always I rested in the afternoon prior to my workout. However there was a price to pay. The next day I would be achy from the activities, my muscles tender, in discomfort.

Later I realized my diet was not good enough to repair and rebuild me. For one, my calorie intake was not sufficient. There was no concentration of critical nutrients needed to rebuild me. This was my next area to concentrate on.

I started taking dietary supplements. These included vitamin B complex twice a week, Maca, a high value root raised in the Andean forests, and Amino acid supplements. There was a slight improvement, or was it a placebo effect? All these changes took weeks, so nothing dramatic occurred.

In the rehab program, my strides were profound, considering where I had started. I was still 145 pounds and lean. My belt held up my pants still. T-shirts hung from my frame. Yet my appetite was not there for muscle growth. A lot more calories would need to be consumed rich in protein, low in certain types of fats and a balanced amount of carbohydrates, with the necessary micro nutrients.

It was almost nine months later. I had kept a low profile but was slowly raising my game, imperceptibly. There was a lot more stamina for life's daily activities and, with adequate rest, some for exercise and rehab. I had indeed come a long way from my bench mark, my chaperoned showers. My conversations with God were tempered now. Still it was a one-sided discussion.

Two wonderful foods came along to actually make me feel like I had eaten well. The first was my mother's chicken soup.

Made of total concern, pieces of chicken, with the bones attached, lots of spices including turmeric, garlic, dash of chili powder, onions, ginger, and lots of things that mothers hold dear to my heart. It was what the doctor ordered. It was served hot in a raised round blue bowl with a slice of crusty bread. Thick in its consistency, it fortified my insides the minute it made contact with my viscera. It was savored to the last drop as was every bowl presented to me. Some foods nourished my heart more than anything. It would stop skipping around every now and at night seemed to beat a little less hard. Indeed my taste buds came alive, and overall it helped my appetite.

The next delicacy was my wife's lassi. This is a drink native to the subcontinent, I believe. Made to be served on the hottest days of the year, it nourishes, cools, and is best enjoyed with close friends.

Back home every vendor had a special way of spinning the ladle that made the mixture and each had his own following. Lassi is made from, ice, milk, yogurt, sugar, and a pinch of salt. Occasionally mango puree may be added. The ingredients are poured into a steel vessel and a wooden ladle with sharp ridges and vigorously rotated for several minutes until there is a white froth head. It is so refreshing on those warm muggy Indian evenings when solid foods are too heavy and the stomach is growling. In America they make it in a dang-founded contraption called a blender. Seems to take something away.

A tall glass of lassi after a cycle ride or the gym was refreshing, hydrating, energizing. This was what I had been craving. What else would I have served if I was back in my make believe castle? And I lusted again that of which I had been deprived for so long!

13

HAWAII VACATION

Tired from a grueling year spent partially in tears, exhaustion, small calamities, and fires that had to be put out I had reached the end of my tether. Even rehab had lost its luster and had become a chore. It had become repetitive, boring, and my muscles and body did not want to respond to therapy. Sleep had become intermittent and not reviving. Mornings were dull, and lackluster food had lost its appeal. It also became a chore to keep my nutrition up. My energy level was near an all-time low. Work was dragging, repetitious. Many small issues kept raising their heads and kept the waters murky. Maybe the struggle was finally going to do me in. Depression was my constant companion, and hopelessness was not far away.

Later that year, while still early into the boys' summer holidays, Doreen one day handed me a manila folder. Inside was an itinerary for our vacation to Hawaii, set to start in a week.

"where did the money come from?"

"Does it matter?"

"No. Yes. Well, I don't know."

She volunteered that the money was from funds set aside for unexpected activities and that the vacation would deplete it much.

For once I did not question the expense or intent but rather looked forward, secretly longing to be there right now. All work and no play, etc. But now I had to scramble to find coverage while I was gone. Tippy, our pet dog, had to get used to living with someone else for a short while, and someone had to babysit the house.

A few days later we boarded a flight from San Francisco to Kona. Dylan, our nephew and a frequent guest on our trips, was also along. On the surface, he seemed no different after his recent car accident, and it was always good to have all the boys present, as they kept each other occupied.

We stayed on the west side of the island, in the town of Kona. Having spent several days enjoying the activities on this side, we prepared for the highlight of the vacation, a trip to the volcanoes and jungle adventures afterward. I was going to use this opportunity to explore more of the island. There were two ways to get to our initial destination, the city of Hilo: straight over the top, or the long way around through a town called Wimea.

Newcomers that we were, we took some advice and traveled the latter route, which took us away from the usual tourist traps and high-priced food to places where there still working ranches and quaint, cozy towns that sold homemade ice cream. Much moisture was in the air as we set out very early that morning. The forests, foliage, altitude, and fragrances from flowering blooms were intoxicating and set the stage for an unforgettable adventure.

On the other side we were introduced to a gentleman who served as our guide to investigate the lava fields further. We entered areas that perhaps we shouldn't have, which we blamed on smoke from vents in the ground that hid signs telling us to keep out.

Soon into our trip the adventures began. The ground under our feet seemed to tremble, or maybe it was the uneven surface that made us unsteady. The soles of our shoes felt warm. Steam vents hissed from the ground in the distance. The smell of rotting eggs permeated the air, wrinkling our noses. Hydrogen sulfide, no doubt, formed somewhere within the volcanic activity and mixed with steam and other noxious fumes.

Low groans were heard as well as felt, but from no obvious source. From this short walk we got to appreciate the fury of hell. Not too far away yellowish red rocks radiated with heat, making us rub our skin frequently. These red rocks seemed to be moving, as we were looking at lava and molten rock at maybe three thousand degrees centigrade in temperature. Was hell that hot?

The hot breezes dehydrated us rapidly. Our water canteens rapidly emptied. We spotted more vents with more lava tubes rushing furiously toward the sea. There the awesome battle of heat and water took place. Plumes of steam hissed into the air from the waves as the liquid rock solidified. This process causes the island to grow and after many, many years, the hot magma turns into luscious forests. Now we noted the origin of the rumbles. They were caused by the lava flowing below us, which we were unaware of initially.

Weak of heart, knocking knees, a dry mouth, and my wife's nail digging into my forearm all caused us to retreat. So this was a rendition of Dante's inferno. It was sobering in its fury, and this was but a glimpse of what was really there. I was privileged to witness the fury of the creation of earth, the same process that gave rise to the Garden of Eden eventually.

We retreated to our transport and back into town we went. There was much activity that needed to be done, and it was not yet noon. We ate snacks at roadside vendors, savored the frozen ice cones, and checked our bearings to our next adventure—zip lining in the forest. A word of advice: don't do it.

High in the canopy gliding over murderous water falls, the jagged spikes of rock would flay us alive if the rope broke or worse cripple us for life. Foolishly on a dare, I decided to join the adventure. A man should know his limits, and clearly I did not know mine. I was going to pay for my fool hardiness. Donning safety harnesses, we got onto jeeps that took us up steep winding paths to the start of this madness. We kept going up , up, and up.

On the first platform, our petite energetic instructor singled me out for extra attention (read: senior citizen care). Looking at the rope as it stretched to the next platform, all was good. I was barely thirty feet above a pasture. Easy yes? Nope! As you launch yourself and speed picks up, the wind whistles in your ears and the ground rushes past you at an alarming rate. Any motion and you start to spin. To slow down, you stretch out your arms and legs and come in for a clean landing. When I spun, I became nauseated. I looked down, got vertigo, and came in backwards for a clumsy landing, jarring my body from the impact. Judging by the jeers, I was quite the source of entertainment for the group. While the kids hung upside down as they zipped down the line and landed the same way, I wondered if my sons were not primates. So the first platform conquered, we started on the segment. Stupid of me!

I was bruised but still a glutton for punishment. Of course the hoots from the boys didn't help. I would have backed out of the second quarter-mile run, but a pressure in the middle of my back sent me whizzing down over a chiasm. Jagged rocks stood to impale me if I slipped. Losing focus, I came in too fast, backwards, and stiff—all no-no's. Bam! I hit the tackle at the receiving end. A rock popped into my mouth and nestled in my cheek. I tasted blood. Enough of this foolhardiness, I quit. Yet the rest of the party came down whooping and hollering, making it seem easier than the one before them. The kids were out of the will. They would pay.

The pebble in my mouth turned to be a piece of tooth. I had bitten down too hard and shattered something. There was no pain, other than my bruised ego. I rode back down to the base camp while the others continued rappelling. At camp I had time to explore the forest up closely and meander down many animal-made trails. A hundred yards from the lodge, one sharp turn and I was alone in the foliage. It was so easy to become disoriented. There were many fruits hanging on vines and laying on the ground. Guavas with red fruit within were to be broken off the stems and bitten into releasing their sweet essence. Coconuts were full of refreshing juice to be had by cracking the nut against a sharp tapered piece of rock making it surrender its elixir. Creeks ran everywhere. Orchids blossomed on the banks. Their delicate structure was so translucent that you could almost see through them. They were like birds of paradise except rooted to one spot. Then I heard the whoops and yells get louder. The group was nearing the end of their adventure.

They all perfected their landings—upside down, legs splayed out, hands outstretched, giving each other the finger. They crashed into the final wooden tackle coming to a rather abrupt halt. Sweaty, scratched, with grime and rope burns, they'd had a most excellent adventure. Now it was time to feed the beast within.

Down in Hilo, we went to a Hawaiian restaurant that served up spicy tacos from Hawaiian fish, and Mexican margaritas made with loni koi juice, from a local fruit. Throw in burritos, whole fried fish, spicy finger foods, and local fresh juices and it was a feast better than the twenty-five-dollar steaks stateside. The food here was cheap and plenty. We were refreshed and battered. Insect bites, scratches, rope burns, all kept us active with our fingers. We were rested now but still feasting on local varieties of ice cream and frozen ices, which came in colors from purple to bright orange. We planned out the rest of the day: get back to our condo and soak in the Jacuzzi to ease all those knotted muscles, then a hot shower to wash off the day's tokens.

Back in the jeep, we were sweaty and tired but exhilarated. We were warriors for the day and had earned our accolades. Mentally we were still swinging from the trees. With the boys now in the back and the wife beside me, we started on our long journey home. The daytime heat had almost left and faint wisps of cool air occasionally stroked our cheeks. Spurred by another crazy impulse, I veered off our itinerary and went for the route over the middle of the island.

"We aren't on the same road we took coming," said one of the observant bunch. "Where are we going, Dad?"

"Thought I'd try the Saddle Road back to Kona."

"Isn't it winding and slow?"

"Probably, but we may never come this way again forever. Let's do it, otherwise I will regret losing this opportunity, and we might even get a glimpse of the observatory."

"Hmmmph, big deal."

"Zip it up and take a nap."

Nondescript comments followed. As the route showed up on the GPS, we picked up the pace just a bit. These were unfamiliar roads and the terrain varied. As we left the town behind, the road lent itself to some aggressive driving. The boys knew I was a frustrated Formula 1 driver. I stepped it up a notch again and started climbing the first set of hills, one of many that headed into the heart of the island.

The road is so named because it starts on either side of the island at the coasts and from either side it climbs gradually through different layers of vegetation and scenery. The weather becomes cooler, less humid, and the sun's rays tingle on the skin at the higher altitudes.

At the oceans fringes the vegetation is densely intertwined. Various plants unknown to me with wide long leaves and delicate fibers running through them adorned the roadside. There were thick vines that jutted abruptly into our path, and small dense green bushes with tiny flowers hid in nooks and crevasses. All this mixed with dense undergrowth could be blamed if one thought it was one of the gardens in paradise. As one ascends, the vegetation thins out and becomes less thick and more verdant. Heading into the setting sun, rounding a sharp turn, one might get blinded by sharp rays of light. Only a moment later it would become dark again driving through a thick patch of foliage pierced by shafts of light. So one may see sun, clouds, rain bursts, blue sky, and fog all within a couple of minutes. At the crest of many mountain ranges, the setting sun bathes the island with its evening shades of golden red and yellow. It hangs in the sky, a glowing orb slowly sinking into the waters far away and extinguishing itself in the huge Pacific Ocean. As the last rays fade away, the waters turn red reflecting light off the crests of waves in the middle of the ocean. Occasional pleasure boats race, not knowing that they were participants on nature's canvas; This panoramic view could be seen only on the higher ridges, and the timing has to be right. The gods had favored me this day. I had seen hell, and now the heavens were displaying their majesty just for me. The colors slowly turned dusky, in preparation for the third part of the canvas—the night sky.

I had chosen well for this day this trip, this road and the timing. The city lights and sights fade as you gain altitude. The commercialized Hawaii fades into the distance. There are rapid switch backs, lazy curves, sharp grades up and down, mixed with more turns and unpredictable weather that changes every few yards at the higher altitudes. As one comes to the middle of the island, the road is at its highest, about 6500 feet. The ground now holds only scrub, miniature trees stunted by a lack of fertile soil and brush. The brown color of the rock is evidence that this island was formed by volcanic activity. At the highest point a dirt road takes off for another 5000 feet to reach the observatory.

Driving this road you must be on guard at all times to enjoy the spectacle unfolding before you. Even as we cruised on the straight ways, the flat rays of the sun blinded me suddenly. Changing gears rapidly to respond to the challenges, my foot went to work: slow down as you approach the turn, accelerate through it, and let momentum take you into the next quick thrill. Tires squeal, gusts of wind buffet the vehicle. The road stays narrow. If you veer off more than a few inches, the crunched gravel reminds you to regain focus. Fog, clouds, and wet patches from rain make regaining your footing that much more challenging. But I had the full measure of this road by now and was going to enjoy every inch of it.

As we climbed further the vegetation thinned out even more. An extensive panorama lay before and below us. Clouds raced across lofty peaks. Remnants from the sun's dying rays gave them a faint tinge of embers.

It was cool outside and a crack in the window let in fragrances emanating from many miles away. We hummed along. The boys had fallen asleep, succumbing to exhaustion and post prandial hyperglycemia. Laying their heads on each other's shoulders, their heads and torso moving in unison with the vehicle. Gently they swayed in the turns, occasionally opening their eyes to see where they were and then drifting off again into slumber. My wife tried to keep me company, yet her eyelids slowly descended, sending her off into a slumber as well. I was alone in my thoughts and for the moment preferred it that way. The radio cut off and silence became more omnipresent.

The landscape became sparser the further and higher we went. There were abrupt banks of fog that blanketed the road, making me slow down. Day had given way to dusk, which was quickly changing to the hues of night and deepening with each minute. Soft grunts and snorts came from the back seat. When the weather broke, faint stars shone through briefly obscured by racing puffs of clouds. More appeared shortly and became brighter. There was a concentration of stars further down, making for constellations that existed only in my head. They twinkled brightly, distant beacons that lead to who knows where. The coast was hidden in the distance. It grew darker. A light drizzle spread moisture on everything in its path. We were near the top of the road midway between the two coasts, and the cutoff was a short distance away.

"Come visit with us," the stars beckoned in unison. I looked at the firmament. They were diamonds embedded in the heavens above, crystal clear. They grew in number, their brightness casting a faint glow on the earth.

"Rest awhile; take a break," they beamed. My family was fast asleep. No one else heard the whispers that curled within my ears. Of its own volition my foot lightened on the pedal. I would never get this opportunity again. Why not? I smiled withi; something of an imaginary bucket list item would be fulfilled. The windows were cold and the heater had come on some time ago, yet it stayed cool. There we were at the turnoff. Rapid fire I downshifted crunching the sand under the wheels. As the car skidded to a stop in a small patch of dirt, the wind whipped dust and tiny gravel along.

"Are we home yet? it's still dark outside."

"Nope, not at home". We are at the top of a mountain and everybody out. Let's have a look see. The sky is awesome. "Move."

Lots of groans and moans followed, yet I persisted. We may never come this way again.

"It's freezing."

"Yup, wrap some blankets around you."

As they straggled out and I turned off the headlights, the night sky lit up as if a switch had been thrown. The cold air sent a shiver through the group. I was expecting more complaints and surprised to hear none. The display was dazzling. The Milky Way stretched above us in a band from ocean to ocean. Stars of all colors and shapes were on display, and there were dark bands of nothing that wove through this palette accentuating the brightness of the stars. Faint streamers, gossamers of silk and satin, wove their way on the canvas. Astronomers may have words for these entities, like intergalactic dust, nebulae, active gas clouds, and so forth. But it was so much more romantic to see them as the work of a supernatural being of a force beyond our own understanding.

There was complete silence from the motley crew. They were in awe. Necks craned upwards to see objects seen in the city with only a fraction of the brightness. Here they were revealed in all their majesty. Stars were blue, red, orange, and all other colors; even the whites had different hues. The North

Star gave me a compass. Constellations were out in force. The Big Dipper seemed resting on a hook waiting to be plucked and dipped.

Off to the left was the Northern Cross among many others. It was bright enough to read a large print magazine. The wind continued to sting with the grit in it. It was close to freezing, and my family had had enough. Good as it was, they wanted back to warmth and shelter of the car. I hope the stop left a memory on their mind. I soon found myself alone.

"let them go, stay awhile," the heavens beckoned. "We have been waiting for you."

The tears started, and sobs wracked my body. My hair stood on end as I sauntered away from the car. The wind whipped me pushing me along, dew condensed on my face; fog partially obstructed and blurred my view. Small objects bounced along reverberating from the mountain walls. I heard sounds like tiny rodents scampering away; there was evidence of small mammals. My eyes watered uncontrollably, whether from emotion or grit I don't know. As more sand stung my body, wearing only summer clothes, it made my skin hypersensitive. All five of my senses were in the hyper-acute phase, including taste, from our gastronomic adventures. My emotions were also raw, not unlike my surroundings. Was I being impressed? No. Instead I felt benevolence; someone understood my plight but could not act. As I meandered away, the shape of the car was obscured by the fog temporarily. The heavens smiled on me. The light and colors from above shone through the mist giving the sky a hue I'd never seen before. There was a feeling of peace and fulfillment. For a moment there was an unobstructed view of the heavens again.

Someone fell in step beside me. The sound was familiar. I did not have to look. There was an immediate kinship. My mind felt free to express itself. There had been much to say, but no one seemed to understand the internal trauma I had faced. I had been alone in my long struggle to recuperate and still was not sure I would make it.

"Is it you old friend? Did you arrange this, did you bring me here?" We needed no introductions. The last time we met I had been afraid. On this occasion I felt a complete bond. No one understood me as much as he did. It was freezing; the cold wind had chilled me to the bone but I could take it. Here was a missing part of me.

"Where have you been? There has been no one to talk to. I have suffered much alone. There has not been much company. My suffering has gone on too long. I have tried repeatedly but not made much progress. The emotional scars do not heal. Could you not have taken me earlier? I have given it everything with not much to show for it. Where do I go from here?

"I may make it, but it has been too rough. There is no map to follow. I don't want anymore. I've done what I can do so far, but I'm so weak there is not much left. I've given it my best, but I'm tired. I carry this façade all the time that all is well. Let me rest some, give me a chance. I can't do much more. Please lift some of this burden."

He kept pace with me but said nothing. The fog was thick and visibility was almost zero. Yet the winds whipped me with sandy grit, my toes were abraded rubbing against rocks, and my naked fingers were numb. I continued my stroll. Someone understood my situation, yet he would not reply. We walked shoulder to shoulder, closer than ever before.

My wife's voice called me in the distance, but I didn't reply.

"It's okay to speak to me," I mentioned, yet nothing but silence.

"Why do you still continue my trial? I am not as strong as you think. I want to live again. And while you're at it, could you take care of a few other problems as well? Give me a sign of what needs to be done. I am floundering all the time, and no one understands. There is no one to reach out to."

I rested against the rock outcroppings, exhausted. My tears were spent; my feelings set sail on the wind taken away from me. I was done for now. Yet I could not say if I was happy or sad at this very moment. My journey resumed, there was silence within, turmoil outside. As the gravel crunched, I willed myself to continue walking in silence.

I felt myself walking alone again. My friend had wandered off, yet his presence accompanied me. The universe was so big above me. How could anyone be concerned about my lot? I was insignificant in the big picture but I demanded so much. I was deluding myself that anyone cared for my lot.

Again the skies cleared. The heavens spread over me benevolently, but I could discern no message. Still, something had been accomplished. I turned toward the car.

"What does Dad see in the stars? I think he makes it all up," said the youngest.

The others complained about everything else. My wife called my name again and my soft reply carried to her, "be there in a minute."

A foot behind them, I wiped the last of the tears away, cleared my throat and with frozen fingers pulled the door ajar.

"Where did you go? You were gone for so long."

It had been fifteen minutes, but I felt like only a minute had elapsed. I had gotten a lot off my chest—maybe.

I took one last look at this spot, burnt it into my mind, and moved on. I was fortunate to appreciate the scene that had unfolded expressly for my benefit. It would sustain me for many years to come.

As the car sprang to life the heater and lights came on, I felt the cold that had sunk into me. I was trembling. Was it from hypothermia or my recent visit? I felt like someone had listened. It had been difficult to relate my situation to ordinary mortals like myself. It took a supernatural presence to understand my plight, though he had not said a word. Going forward would be easier.

Back on the road, I glanced one last time at the spot. Were the rocks deceiving, or was there an outline of a figure against a wall jumbled with other formations?

"Yes, old friend, let's meet again." The scenery changed again, and there was darkness.

"Were you talking to yourself again?" Doreen asked.

"Yes. I'm going loony tunes; Probably will need a straight jacket one of these days."

She laid her hand on my arm and rested. The family was boisterous in the back, mainly grouching at me. My nephew seemed impressed at the colors of the stars and their sizes. Betelgeuse was clearly visible as was Sirius. As I picked up speed we crested the final ridge and now were on the east side of the island. We had crossed the halfway mark. Kona itself lay like a distant star almost in the sea yet not quite.

The moon that had chased the sun across the sky for most of the day now burst its reflected light across the top of the ocean, accentuating the white caps of the crashing waves. A vibrant beam shone from the west to east, bathing the landscape with its scintillating brilliance. Was my friend sending me a message? Was he illuminating the way? His actions spoke more eloquently than words could describe. I felt his presence around me.

As we picked up speed on a straightway, a lazy turn at a sharp curve made me brake hard; tires squealed as they navigated the change. Wet patches of asphalt made me grip the wheel harder waiting for the skid. Abrupt banks of clouds slowed my momentum down again. Patches of moonbeams illuminated other parts, encouraging me on. The gods themselves would have enjoyed the race in their chariots. As we approached the coast, the voices of my family became faint until there was no one but me.

I drifted into a dialogue with myself. It seemed to summarize all of life's experiences and compared them to one day's adventures. To me the most traumatic part of living is the birthing process. But because of the labor, a baby is born into the world in a rather tumultuous manner. The life grows and matures and spreads its character across its landscape. In due time life gives birth to new life, and the process continues.

Was not the volcanic activity we had witnessed a similar process? Molten rock gave birth to these wonderful islands lush with life. The islands grew from nubbins to their present size. Were we not crawlers ourselves, once barely able to balance? Even as we grow don't we leave ourselves attached to our families and homes by mental tethers? We measure our progress retrospectively by looking at milestones in our history. And each time we venture out, we go a little bit further. Swinging from branch to branch we sometimes get injured and need to be nurtured. We go out but always come back home. And didn't we do just that on the on the zip lining adventure? Securely fastened with ropes and clips, we launched from platform to platform, each time a little bit further and that much faster. Sometimes we were scraped and bruised, but that is the price for our adventures. The line securely held us as we ventured out further each time.

Like our ride full of twists and turns, wet patches, and banks of fog, our lives wander through a panorama of events. Whenever life seems to be going the best, something seems to throw a wrench in the works, and we have to change the direction of our life. The sooner we make the necessary changes; we are back on the road with minimal squealing of tires.

With the best of intention we still skid off the road every now and then. You have to claw back to civilization, changing gears, dropping speed, changing directions repeatedly until the path is apparent again. Sometimes we enter periods of life when we don't know what lies ahead, just like the fog and clouds that obstructed us. We make changes again.

Then there are giant periods that, like the landscape illuminated by the moon, the path is well marked. Everyone is content and the going is good. Savor those moments, isolated as they may seem. For they are rites of passage; The slips and skids are valuable in the lessons they teach us, for in our mistakes and failures we learn the most. Driving down a arrow straight road is boring. Throw in all the above elements and the ride comes alive.

Like my visit at the top of the mountain, on occasion we need to stop and ponder where we are, what have we accomplished, and what lies ahead. A particular incident or individual brings insight to help fill in the blanks and give meaning and strength for the journey ahead. Even as adults, we need our hand held on occasion, for we all get overcome with that around us. Finally, when life calms down, as the road straightens, we have navigated the worst and can enjoy the just rewards of our labor.

My recent experience tested most of these paradigms, and they seemed to fit the reality of my life, which had been full of roller coaster experiences. Finally there were signs that it was smoothing out again.

We continued to drive through the landscape we had witnessed from above. What had seemed mystical was now real and we were a part of that reality. The town grew larger as we approached. The night sky and tantalizing landscape vanished; ranches and tracts of homes appeared. We rolled into town, my muscles ached, and my body felt it was still vibrating from the car ride. A most excellent shower followed with more food and drink. Our wounds were now attended to, cuts and abrasions were disinfected, Band-Aids put on with a kiss. Finally laying down with my wife, the boys, who had rested, now came to life. On came the video game Gran Turismo, and the sound of racing cars pierced the walls of the living room. As I fell asleep, I was now the passenger for that brief moment between drowsy and sleep when he was driving the car. Ah yes, the boys had been with dad all along.

The next day, it was time to go home. The thoughts of the vacation had not crystallized yet. That would happen later. For now I lived to enjoy and savor the moment. It had been a long barren spell.

Landing back stateside, I was exhausted by the trip. Even relaxation has its price. I was more tired than when I had started. But the many experiences I had encountered would keep me busy for some time. I knew I would recover. To bring me back to myself, I had to fall back on my skills of resting, adequate sleep, good nutrition, and gentle exercise even though my muscles ached. I kept my thoughts to myself, to be sorted out and made sense of later. Many real issues needed to be resolved and wrapped up. This vacation was but a brief interlude.

14

WHO IS CONRAD CASTELLINO? AN IMMIGRANT'S STORY

I have to be one of the most complicated identities on the earth, reality on par with a fictional personality. It could be the stuff of espionage, stolen identity, or a schizophrenic with a multiple personality disorder. How can it be that a Catholic lived in Pakistan and calls it his home country as much as any other Pakistani? How could he have such a Westernized name; surely he has made this up to blend in the West and hide his true identity. But wait, he looks like he might be from the Caribbean and speaks with a British accent. To hear him speak and his mannerisms, you might think he graduated from an English boarding school. Here was a real conundrum. So we take a break from the non-stop stress of living in the West and take a short stroll down memory lane, which is a long way away.

I am the fifth among eight siblings. I was born at Holy Family Hospital, Karachi, Pakistan in 1960 and was baptized at St. Patrick's Church. About 1 percent of 150 million people are of a religion other than Islam. There are Christians, Hindus, Parsis, and other minority religions. /

I went to St. Patrick's High School, as did most of my siblings. My sister went to St. Josephs convent. We grew up in the heart of downtown Karachi, in a district called Saddar. As a young lad there was much to admire in the city, particularly landmarks, parks, and other structures built during the time of British rule. We grew up not really caring that we were a minority. We enjoyed the cultures around us. There were so many ethnic groups, each with their own culture yet living side by side with others. My friends and those of my family's were from all walks of life. There was no overt talk of "us versus them." We enjoyed each other's festivals, like Eid, Holi, and Christmas. Gifts were exchanged between families, obligatory visits were made. Alcohol was served discreetly to those so inclined to drink. No one forced their views on anyone else. Minorities played a major role in the country's growth since independence in 1947. Many minorities were entrepreneurs. The Parsis come to mind in this regard. Catholics held many coveted posts in various branches of the government. The first mayor of Karachi was a Catholic and a friend of my father's. Minorities held their own and were respected for their consistency, hard work, ethics, and dedication.

As time passed, the old order of things changed. Merit and hard work were not criteria for selection; rather it became who you know and where you came from. I was lucky to leave while there was still relative peace and harmony. Since then, regional conflicts and the meddling of foreign powers are destroying what was the natural harmony of the region. We now anxiously wait to see what will transpire next. I was friends with many school mates with whom I still keep in touch. It didn't make a difference what faith they belonged to.

Originally my parents and grandparents came from the south of India. They came to Pakistan for economic opportunity. My great, great, great grandparents converted to Catholicism. Prior to that they would have been Hindus.

Allow me to digress and give a brief history of the spread of Christianity in the Indian subcontinent. Back in the 1500s, Vasco de Gama, a Portuguese explorer, was among the first chaps to find a route from Europe to India by going around southern Africa and running north for several thousand miles. He landed in southwest India and later established a Portuguese colony called Goa. This served as a portal for trade with the locals. They were followed by the Dutch India shipping lines and the British.

Along with trade and commerce came missionaries wanting to convert the local wretches to eternal freedom. That work could be provided to the converts and assistance such as living on the farms helped the conversion along. To separate the converts from the heathens, we were given names that came from the country of our benefactor. So I would presume my ancestors were converted by a priest from a Mediterranean country, which would explain our last name, Castellino. The first names were also similarly allotted. Naming a child after a saint was especially apropos. So I was named Conrad Joachim Michael Castellino.

The Goans proved adept at clerical work and other supporting roles, thus they found employment in many of the British colonial institutions. The small Goan community spread to diverse corners of the British empire, including some to Karachi, a sleepy seaport of twenty-five thousand people to which my grandparents immigrated in the 1930s. They were part of a migration that today has reached the shores of America.

In Karachi, my grandfather worked as a tiffin wallah. He made midday meals with a Goan and Mangalorean flavor and delivered them to offices in the business district. Thus wives were freed up and husbands at offices got home-cooked meals. Today they are known as Dabbawalas in India.

Alas this was not high class, as I was reminded by members of my community back home. But food never tasted as good when I sat in my grandfather's lap sipping his soda and gym-khana whisky and snacked on foods made that day for others. Today I'm sure my grandfather is proud of his progeny and what we have accomplished. My mind to become a physician was made up when he fell in ill health for several years and would ask me when would I become a doctor.

Immigrating to the United States in the mid-1980s, we settled on the West Coast. It was the land of opportunity, hot dogs, pizza, McDonald's, and chicks in bikinis where no one seemed to really work. Most of my family had come before me; my eldest brother had come to Georgetown University on a scholarship in 1969, when I was nine years of age.

As I studied for the qualifying exams that would let me into a residency, I tried my hand at many skilled trades. I made tacos, baked bread, watched over private property, and finally cleaned dishes in a hospital. After passing my exams I found myself on the East Coast for my residency. It was rough and heartless being on call every other night. Initially in Washington D.C., subsequently I moved to upstate New York to complete my training. The stories you hear of residents are mostly true, and mine was not much different. Yet challenging as it was I think a certain length of time needs to be spent in an intense environment.

Life goes on 24/7 and so does sickness. Spending long hours in a hospital trains you to follow the progression of diseases in a way you never would if it was a nine-to-five occupation. It is a rite of passage for a doctor, and there is no way around it if you want to be an MD.

Doreen joined me after a few years while I was still in training. My regret is that being so engrossed in my studies, there was no room for anything else into my life. I could have done a better job preparing my wife for our new home.

After training we moved to a quaint town near Yosemite National Park in the Sierra Mountains. It deluded me of my impression of small-town America, where everyone was supposed to have white picket fences and apple pie on the kitchen window ledge. Still we settled in the heart of California that has been home for a decade or so.

I worked hard at my profession. Maybe the best compliment I ever received was, "that SOB will take of you, no matter what is interfering in your care."

It took a long time to tone down my macho ways, a toning down that was helped along by my health issues. Today I practice as I used to, but with less intensity. I allow more time to relax and work out. But I still have not learned to let go fully when away from work.

As a retired physician once mentored me said, "Two years after you quit working, if the phone rings in the middle of the night, you still think it's the emergency room on the other end."

What makes physicians so hard? Self-immolation is really not in our style, but yet we persist. We start with twelve years of very competitive schooling. To most of us, it starts around the tenth grade when we initially decide what our field is. In college, every classmate is also competition for the same spot in medical school. After numbing pre-medical studies and a survival-of-the-fittest competition with the Medical College Admission Test, a few of us finally make it into medical schools. Then onto three years of training called a residency program; Finally, we get to practice in one of the primary care fields like family practice or internal medicine, among others. Along the way we're told to be compassionate and feel others' suffering. But our training is anything but humane. Humiliation, razing, and questioning are standard in teaching medicine. Thus one comes out scarred and bruised, despite the "humane" message. Yet strange as it seems, when you have the responsibility of maintaining life, you have to believe in yourself to the max. Otherwise it is simply incomprehensible to discharge such duties. To me, foreign graduates with lesser standards back home compete with the best of Ivy League graduates. I spent many years in private practice, which is now a quickly dying field. I worked many long hours. I never got to the proverbial Wednesday afternoon golf game. Many of my colleagues worked even harder than I did. After the day was done, and after dinner at home, it was a trip to the hospital to do my evening rounds; As my youngest son told his mom, "Dad doesn't come home till the sun goes down."

During the night, it was standard to get a call or two, but that's light for an internist and its specialties. When on call for a group, sometimes the need arose to make night visits to the hospital and resume work the next day in a normal manner.

Even then some doctors find time to dabble in other affairs on the side. It is a continuation of residency and the ingrained belief that work is good and more work is better.

At that time, the real estate market in my town was sky-rocketing. The natural thing to do was to invest. This was to prove my success and my undoing.

Should I have done it differently? Well the whole damn country was investing in real estate and stocks. You were a damn fool if you didn't participate. Business centers were opening all over the place; mom and pop entrepreneurs were starting on ventures on their own. Nothing could go wrong. How could it? People from major metropolitan areas were moving here, the projected growth rate doubled and this was heaven for our depressed nook in the woods.

Then the heavens opened. Overnight it seemed the world collapsed around us. Housing prices started to tumble and picked up speed with every passing week. You could not move fast enough if your life depended on it. Calamity and catastrophes were all around us. Throw in failed businesses, and you have all the ingredients for the perfect storm, though mine was perhaps a tad more severe. Thus on March 3, 2008, my predicament began.

15

AND GOD TOLD THE HEAVENS TO POUR SOME MORE

Back stateside after vacation, issues kept raising their heads. Don't ever go for a vacation to rest. That is a made-up concept to keep us going. The physical demands on my strength persisted, taxing whatever activity I undertook. A workout was still not pleasurable; it was too much of a chore, and the aches afterwards lasted for several days.

My dialogue with God persisted: What was the lesson for me here? Why me? What was expected of me? There were no replies, no matter how often I pleaded.

My feelings of imminent death had faded. I knew I was allowed to live, but the feeling that I had to have a major direction change in my ideals, goals, and what I wanted to be remembered for after my mortal remains had been interred and my soul wandered in the fields of Elysium. Looking back, it was a period of guidance that emanated from my innermost self. Was it my conscience or my subconscious? One was spiritual the other was cerebral. When would I be able to comprehend the new direction that was already there for me? The straight path I had walked down earlier came to mind.

Issues of the real world always seemed to get in the way of an understanding that was more ethereal. The crushing oppression was lifting, but just a tad. I could breathe and contemplate living in the physical world again, but it would take more time, recovery, strength before I could enjoy some of the rewards.

So at this time my wife was ready to strangle somebody, justly so. In our attempts to refinance our house we contacted our bank. We cannot modify, they said. We know of your situation, but you don't fit our criteria. Many appeals followed with the same stonewalling. Finally on advice from some in the industry, I stopped making my payments. Many threats followed: loss of home, eviction, bad credit, etc.

Yet I stood my ground. We would like to refinance. Finally we were asked to submit a summary of our financial status and fill up umpteen forms. Many documents had to be updated again and again. Finally we called to find out the status of the refinancing.

"There is no file on your property, sir. We have no documentation on file."

So we started the process again. More documents and updates went to the loan company. After a period of time, we called back. They had our file, but our loan was now with Penny Mac. We would have to contact them. Would we like their number?

After taking time to cool down we contacted the new loan company. Initially the loan was with one agent, and things progressed stutteringly. Duplicate documentation was needed when the initial copies were lost, misplaced, or not legible. Then after some more time, silence again and a phone call.

"Yes, we have your file, but the agent on the case has changed. Your new contact is (take a deep breath, have a drink)."

This is impossible. How is this bail-out program supposed to work? The system was geared with impossible bureaucracy. It was not my understanding of how the system was supposed to work. They were supposed to be helping out.

After sitting in the freezer for several weeks cooling down, we again contacted the loan company and spoke to our agent.

"Let me find your file and get back to you," which she did. So we limped along with no particular conviction that we'd get anything accomplished. Finally enough documentation had been submitted, and we would know the outcome in the near future.

We received an offer of a reduction of principle and an interest rate of 6.5 percent! What? I thought they wanted us to keep our house. This was not the refinance standard that I was made aware of. I persisted in a discussion that the rate was out of the ballpark and I needed to do some research on the issue. There were threats that we would be evicted, and there was no further appeal process. This was it.

"Thank you, yes, I will get back to you. I will consult family members who are in the real estate business."

Two days later another call came. We had qualified for another program, and now our interest rate would be 3.5 percent. Wow! A three-point drop. Maybe there was a God after all. Finally something had gone our way, but it was a bittersweet victory. The process had been so tedious that we almost gave up several times.

The next problem was our car, a new Saturn we had purchased just before my heart attack. The car was actually delivered while I was in a coma. No one was around to receive it, and it was finally it was dropped off at home. It was a total disaster, the repairs had started literally the day after we bought it, and there were many trips since then to fix ongoing problems. There was a faulty battery, then a faulty charging system, engine sensor failure, loose parts in the body paneling, engine leaks, a brake failure at seven thousand miles, and on and on. Whenever we would call to talk to the manager, he was never around. And we called many times. Finally we try contacting Saturn headquarters directly.

"No, we won't change your car. You have too many miles to it."

"Yes, but we started complaining a long time ago. No one paid us heed."

And partially overcome by our other calamities I had put the car on the backburner until more pressing needs were solved.

"Well, you should have contacted us earlier."

"We did for six months, but no one replied to our e-mails except to send us more promotional material."

"It's too late to exchange cars, but if you go into a dealer and buy a newer model, well make sure you get a good deal."

"But why should I buy a car from you after such a bad experience with the car that we have?"

And that was the end of it. That was when we got an extended warranty on the car. We so needed that, because as regular as clockwork the car would go down. The oil spots on the concrete told me that another trip to the dealer was coming up. Now when that car is paid off it will be sold off promptly. It held too many bad feelings with it.

And still we had another minor nuisance to deal with. This one happened earlier and was an example of dealing with bureaucracy at its worse.

At this time I had been concluding my relationship with a business of which I had been the medical director. A letter from Sacramento, the state capital, said I had violated certain business codes and I needed to meet with the department of consumer affairs. We had to hire another attorney to help clarify this.

"Apparently, Doctor," the lawyer explained, "you ran an ad and did not state on it you if the people in the picture were models or clients."

"That's it?"

"Yes."

"I have to attend a formal hearing for that, you're sure?"

Like others who had helped us, the attorney seemed to want to keep things simple and easy for us. He outlined certain strategies for us to follow at the meeting. On the appointed day, with butterflies in my stomach with some staff to keep me company on the drive there and back, we went to meet the executioner. Our lawyer was a gentleman. I had told him of my health problems, but he had no idea how this would play.

Simply, the more fines that were levied the more credit the magistrate got. Plus there was a huge power play, as always with the bureaucracy, to show their might and flex their muscle.

At the meeting my attorney whispered that the judge, a woman, did not seem too accommodating. "Be prepared."

"She looks alright. Maybe she'll understand my situation."

Well, we got nailed on this little piece of legal trivia. Whenever an ad is placed the buyer must specify if the people in the pictures are models or actors. That was it. Open a newspaper and look at how many advertisements are there. Note if any specified if the people in photos are models or clients. If it's not mentioned they are violating California law and subject to loss of business, fines and other remediations. So if one wants to finger a competitor, this is one way of doing so.

And why had we not replied to her summons earlier?

I explained of being hospitalized and comatose. However this back fired miserably.

"Well Doctor Sir, if you were comatose, did you make arrangements for coverage of our patients?"

"Yes, there were several physicians from the community who covered me."

"Do have written agreements with any of these individuals?"

"No. I was in a coma and indisposed afterwards."

"So you have no written agreements, I take it. Doctor, I think I need to open another case on you for abandonment of your clients."

I gave up. I was being toyed with just to stroke someone's ego. I wondered when would it stop. All my anger, rage, frustration, and grief came rolling back. I stayed rock still, unable to trust myself to move or speak.

My attorney stepped in and took control.

"Well and good. We can talk about that later, but let's finish this issue on the table."

Back and forth they went. My attorney held his ground, and no further damage was done. I had to pay a fine, and the judge would get back to us if further charges were going to be filed. Was I really hospitalized, as I had stated? What evidence is there?

I handed over some documents that summarized the events of the last few months, including my hospitalization. She leaned back, and took her time reading the missive.

Where were you hospitalized? How long? And other pleasantries.

"Well, I am sorry that this happened to you, but we have to pursue complaints very seriously. Have a good day." With a nod to the others she was done.

My friend consoled me as we went to his suite and I composed myself.

"That was one of the most bizarre and trivial cases I've ever seen. You were lucky. Someone wanted to malign you, or something else was at play here. Do you have enemies?"

"No enemies, just competition. But no one that I think would do this."

"Are you involved in anything else?"

"I don't think so, but let me double check."

"Can I find out who complained?"

"You can, and you can challenge the decision that was rendered here today, However, let it go. The trial here was ridiculous, spare yourself the trouble and put this behind you, please."

So I did. This one was easy to forget, but boy did I have bad karma. The two-hour ride home was in silence. There was much to reflect on and be bitter about. There was a great hurt within, and I cussed the man upstairs.

"When will you stop this crap? Haven't I had enough? Haven't I done enough these few years to deserve a break? Stop it already!"

Burned out, I let my mind wander. Put this behind you. Nothing major happened and yet another issue has been resolved. The slate is getting cleaner. I looked at the positive. Many issues had been worked through, and slowly my strength was returning. There was sunshine behind the clouds. Hang in there. Hang in there. You will survive. You are around for a reason. *Tranquillo, senor, tranquillo.*

16

THE SCARS OF VICTORY

Work had settled down. I could put in more effort without the attendant exhaustion. Still I took a break from going to do hospital rounds, and I was not involved in extraneous projects. I was working smarter but not harder. I didn't chase down every piece of paper that was missing. I saw the tasks in front of me and took my time and stayed with my duties conscientiously. I ceased to be obsessive about minutia and delegated duties so that my time was more effectively utilized. Having divested myself of my businesses, I truly had free time. The evenings were my own. There were fewer meetings to attend. So I spent more time at the gym and continued to gently increase my activities.

This was the best summer I'd had for a long time. There were plenty of outdoor activities geared towards improving my physical well-being. I spent hours in the warm sun, became sweaty that my T-shirt clung to my back, and got back to a deeper skin shade. There was a rare episode of mild congestive heart failure afterward, so I took the necessary medications and moved on. I didn't call my cardiologist with most problems, knowing how to treat them myself, and I had enough meds at home to open a pharmacy. I would walk further now, up to almost half a mile while stopping every two hundred yards. Workouts were two or three times a week. Afternoon or late evening naps were de rigueur. The afternoon naps were so refreshing, it made me feel like I was awaking up again in the morning. The energy boost was tremendous. Instead of a rundown evening it was upbeat and energized. Food was simple low fat, more protein complex carbs and more fiber. My insides felt the best they had felt in a long time.

The mental battles receded. There were more thoughts of rebuilding myself. A lot of ground had been covered these last few months. Now the momentum had to be maintained.

My birthday came at the end of July. It was a somber moment. This was my third birthday since my MI, and I counted all these milestones dear to me. I had learned that most occasions affected me. I was most conscious that I was not supposed to be here and that every milestone was to be treasured. This birthday I sobbed on the sofa, the one I laid on when I came home from the hospital. I was stronger now and it showed a as I leaned on Doreen's shoulder. My boys, unlike in previous years, got me a present, *The Big Book of the Universe*, full of pictures of various stars, galaxies, nebulae and constellations. The pictures were blown up in color and very vivid. The detail was startling super resolution. The boys presented it to me when I was sobbing. This was the first time they had displayed concern overtly for my condition, and the present reflected foresight on their part. My trip to Hawaii had rubbed off on them. They had given me a book on astronomy, one of my favorite subjects. I treasure that book, always remembering the thought behind it .Many was the night I woke up looked the book over, relived my Kona visit and nursed myself back to sleep.

That week the family took me to buy a bicycle. I had earned it. So off we were testing bicycles. It came to me that I sat on a bicycle whose pedals locked onto your feet into place and could only be released by kicking off to one side. Not knowing this, I wobbled, lost balance, and down I went. I had not even taken a turn of the pedal. I fell on my right side; my right arm, torso, and head hit the concrete less than two inches from my wife's shoe. The shock gave me a vicious jolt that rocketed around my being. I was dazed initially, and felt stupid next. My head spinning and not sure I was coming or going, I was extricated from the bicycle and rested while bemoaning my new fate. I would have a headache in the morning, but the elbow, well I could not extend it the other way fully, and it was slightly swollen. We abandoned the shopping trip and went home to nurse my wounds. It was soon apparent that I had a problem in the elbow. It was throbbing and there was less range of motion. I slept fitfully during the night. In the morning I went to Urgent Care and got an X-ray. It was a mess. The head of a bone called the radius in the forearm had shattered; there was compromise of the whole elbow. I was splinted, narcotics were prescribed, and I went home bummed. Just as things were going full bore again this had to happen. Nothing was going to be handed to me on a platter; I would have to earn it, inch by bloody inch. The next morning I went to have my arm casted. It would stay on for six weeks, and I would be sidelined for at least another three months after the cast came off. There went my routine. Work would be a real problem; I was right-handed and wrote a lot. This was a major setback. All my gains for the year would be eradicated, plus I knew I would likely slip back mentally, reversing many of the gains made to date. The following morning I went to see my bone specialist, and the gods smiled at me.

"Conrad, these days we avoid casting, as it causes muscle wasting and loss of function and strength. Why don't we put it in a padded brace and do a few things so we can make this happen for you?"

This was unbelievable news. I would be able to continue using my right hand, though it would not be fun. Immobility and analgesics for two weeks would control the pain. But no cycling or gym activities for three months minimum and more likely up to six months, except for walking.

Immediately my fragile mood brightened. I could survive this. I was stronger now and thinking more assertively and decisively. This injury showed how fragile my recovery was and how easily it could be derailed. Isn't it so in our personal lives as well? So often things go well only to take nasty turns, and just when the finish line is in sight we can take a spill and lose it all.

I kept my positive spin on it and started walking more at the gym and maintained more consistency. I slowly began to show gains. I could walk farther with less discomfort than before. my elbow throbbed for about a month and then became like a dull toothache for another. I stayed with it, attending to my regular duties while thinking about spending time at home and writing a book on my recent experiences.

Three months later I was cycling again. The throbbing afterward told me I had goofed. Still with liniments, anti-inflammatories, and wraps, I slowly resumed my activities. Summer was in full bloom, the sun was up until almost nine o'clock, and the lassi afterward was always welcome. I was on the road to recovery. I was going to overcome. After everything I had been through, a broken elbow was a walk in the park.

17

QUIT SELF-PITY

I came to the realization that I had wallowed in self-pity for too long. What's done is done is done; let's make sense of it, understand it, reason through it, find a meaning, and move on. If I can't find meaning, I still needed to move on. So a strategy emerged: in my practice, I would concentrate on patients who were in dire need and develop my ability to empathize. I describe empathy as putting yourself in someone else's position, imagining what that person is going through, recognizing the mental trauma, and sharing your own experiences. This may help him or her open up. In the many calls I received after my crises, I knew people were benefiting from my story and relating to my experiences.

Many times I cried with friends shamelessly, and this was a rewarding experience. Most importantly, I had to be comfortable telling my story. Big deal; For seven days I was naked on a table. Was there any need to feel ashamed? No. I was comfortable telling my story, and I decided to relate my experience more often. I firmed up in my mind the decision to write about my experiences.

I reached out to help others and felt that this is my biggest contribution to society. This, I decided, is what the whole shebang was about. But I never would have known it if I had not gone down this crazy path.

Every line of every story held meaning for me now. I felt I could read people more deeply, almost eerily. Mostly I could sense when people had something on their shoulder that they wanted to talk about but didn't know how. Often they were angry, confused, sad, lonely, frightened, and ashamed, had low self-worth, irritable, withdrawn, not given to exuberance, and had repetitive negative thoughts racing through their mind pushing all sane and rational thoughts out of the way. Accompanying these disturbances were concrete medical symptoms, like a constant stiff neck. Headaches starting at the back of the head, difficulty concentrating, forgetfulness, palpitations, and shortness of breath, much like a heart attack; Going to bed exhausted and being wide awake in a few minutes, then tossing and turning the night away left many patients shaken and dazed.

So preoccupied can one become with self-defeating thoughts that one feels that there is no redemption or hope in sight. The problem that many people have is that negative emotions so dominate their thinking that all positive feelings are banished to a dark corner in the brain and kept undercover. Those were the people I reached out to the most. It is easier to listen than to talk when one is so overwhelmed. Even so, someone may still not feel open in talking, but he or she is relieved that someone else has gone down the same path and can overcome great adversity. There is light at the end of the god dammed tunnel.

The more I related the story of my recovery and setbacks, the more I felt at peace with myself. This was a lesson I had learned well, and if it helped others so much, bully for me. I would tell my story.

Around this time, a mutual friend introduced to a woman from the Caribbean who was studying for her qualifying exams. She needed guidance and support. After meeting with her for several months and telling her of my recent struggles, she opened up to me as well. Diana introduced me to her husband. Both he and Diana were badly out of shape. In the few months I had gotten to know her she found out my game plan for recovery was going well and I was going to step it up. My zeal impressed her, she wanted to know if I would work out with her man and get him going again. He had become a couch potato and lost and personal zero motivation.

This was a challenge I needed too.

18

MANUEL

On my first meeting with Manuel, he seemed to hold back. I surmised that he was nervous about being forced to meet me and workout. Yet he seemed willing enough to try. His T shirt size was XXXL, and his body mass index was close to 50. We spoke at length. I asked him what he wanted out of the exercise and weakly he answered to get back into shape and get some of his life back. He was a couch potato to the max but knew he was going down a road of destruction and hardship.

Later he related that based on what his wife had told him, he expected me to be a robust individual. I was the complete antitheses of fitness. I looked older than my stated age. My skin was loose, my color pale, and I was anything but fit. Thus he felt surprised that I was to be his coach. Perhaps my frailty made it easier for him. If I could stick with a game plan, maintain some degree of effort, and just stick with it, then shame on him for backing out.

A very helter skelter relationship developed. I knew from prior workout partners that within a month enthusiasm wanes, and then we revert back to what we were. So I spoke to Manuel about the basics of a workout program, keeping a schedule, and maintaining a diet. We also talked about our commitment and responsibility to each other.

Did he do it? Well, it has been eight months as I write this and we are still at it. Manuel has had substantial weight loss, his attitude has changed for the positive, and he feels that life will be fulfilling after all. Bully for Manuel.

I am proud of this guy for hanging in there. But family obligations, illnesses to close friends, work, and room for other indispensable activities keep us distracted. However, we will regroup soon and re launch on the second phase of our fitness endeavor. Thus a negative has been turned to a positive by designating downtime as a needed rest period.

We started at a local health club. On his first day, Manuel was terrified. There were so many people there, and they all seemed to know what they were doing. He kept a cap on during our whole routine. Shakily we approached the bank of treadmills, and I got Manuel dialed in before his discomfort made him want to leave. He almost tripped as he stepped on the moving belt and shakily took his first step. It was the first of a million more to come. At the slowest speed possible, we started on our journey.

He lasted ten shaky minutes. Any minute I expected him to call it quits, but he stuck it out. We progressed to cable and pulley exercises, stretching most of the muscle groups, upper and lower back, and the chest and arms. After a light workout I told Manuel we had done well. I was happy. I warned him of side effects like sore muscles, headache, dizzy spells. He was fine the next day, and we persisted into a second round. Again he did well. We even played some racquetball, which Manuel loved. He was earnestly sweating and looked wobbly on his feet. But he was breathing hard stuck to his guns.

Much later he told me his initial impression had been that it would be easy to keep up with a fifty-year-old dude who'd had a major heart attack and other health problems. That first day, he had felt his chest was going to explode on the treadmill and his legs felt like giving way beneath him.

I asked him what his motivation was to stick with it, and he earnestly replied that his life was going nowhere. He was facing serious health problems and working out with me not only changed him physically but also turned his life around. He had more energy, was less worried, and generally felt better. It was understood that he was terrified of actually going to the gym and that my presence and support reassured him greatly. He was hiding under his cap as he worked out, seeking anonymity.

But Manuel was gutsy. He stayed with it. Of course, he insisted I was an excellent instructor. Which I was, and will explain later. After running out of a trial membership, we tried out other gyms in town. At each place we got a two-week pass and used it to the max. About three times a week, initially thirty minutes, then forty-five, and finally up to two hours on a good day!

Our routine was simple, but we made a pact to stick with it. Each workout started with twelve minutes of treadmill work, then onto body parts such as chest, arms, thighs, back, and so forth. Rotating different body areas lessened the strain. We made sure we were well hydrated during long workouts to increase lactic acid removal. We maintained this routine for four long months.

Initially Manuel was disappointed when there were no visible results although we had been working out for a month . I reassured him that his metabolic rate was still suppressed and results would start soon. So we started on the culinary part of the workouts. I stressed certain food groups over others, timing of meals, slow release carbohydrates, adequate rest, and always staying positive and focused. This mission was as valuable as digging for treasure. Only consistent hard work would show results.

As time went by we became stronger and the workouts were more fun and enjoyable. Once having been whopped by a girl who obviously lifted more and had much more stamina than us, we threatened to meet her in the parking lot to settle the disrespect. We became good friends and Manuel thrived on his new friendship.

Teaching Manuel actually helped me more than he knew. To stay with him, I had to maintain consistency. Next I had to develop habits that would set an example and model the level of effort for each day. I could not have random heavy workout days that would ruin it for many days to follow. I had to be consistent and lead by example. Manuel needed a steady motivator, and I would not let him down. As he had said, our activities had opened a whole new vista in his life.

We gradually increased the weights we were working with, and one day Manuel related that he had lost three pounds since his last check. This was huge, and I had to now carry the game forward even more. I asked Manuel if he cycled. He hadn't for many years, but he had a bike in the garage somewhere. It was soon cleaned and serviced, and we started on the most enjoyable part of the workouts: bicycling, which is a most wonderful sport. You are outdoors, with fresh air blowing on you, fields rolling by, or traffic. Initially you concentrate on control, getting comfortable sitting on those danged seats, and developing a new set of muscles. Your back is uncomfortably stretched at first, but with more rides it loosens up, and stiffness decreases. Finally you cycle more than four hundred yards at a time, and confidence starts to pick up. Your daily mph rises from four to about ten. Quite reasonable.

Being a techie, Manuel had an app on his iPhone that kept track of his fastest and slowest speeds, calories expended, time spent, route travelled, etc. It gave us concrete evidence that we were improving. We went up to three-mile rides mixing it up with days at the gym. The evenings were long and lent themselves to late afternoon rides when the heat was not intense.

Then the wives got into it. On our first few rides we ate some traditional Pakistani food, which Manuel and his wife thoroughly enjoyed. They took their respective men home as warriors, which we didn't mind too much.

Our persistence continued. With Manuel's change in diet, the weight kept coming off. He shed one or two pounds every week. Of course there were weeks when none came off, but I reassured my friend when things didn't go as planned. Stick with it, and when nothing else worked I pulled out the pity card.

"Look, you dipshit, I didn't have this heart attack for nothing. You got to put back what I gave to you. I call in some of my markers."

He gave in, perhaps happy at my persistence, I suspect. Later I told him I would send a bill for all my coaching and he said he would gladly pay if he had any funds. He did agree that if medicine failed, I could become a life coach. Five months into our workout people were commenting I was looking well, looking fitter and healthier.

More importantly on Manuel's Facebook site he was receiving compliments on how well he was coming along and asking about his secret, to which he replied, "hard work, diet, and a nut named Conrad."

We both faced many challenges. My practice was still being rebuilt. I fatigued easily and needed afternoon naps to face Manuel in the evening. The health of Manuel's parents was failing, and they needed frequent hospitalizations.

When faced with such situations we went into maintenance mode. We made little progress, but we maintained a certain level of activity so that inertia would not sideline us completely.

After eight months, Manuel had dropped forty pounds. I had gained ten pounds of muscle and a total of fifteen pounds since starting my workouts. That was impressive. My strength and stamina had increased, my mood improved, and the more I exercised the better I felt and slept.

Many obstacles remain for both of us, but we have committed to step it beyond out plateau and just bully on through all of life's challenges.

19

HOW TO SURVIVE WHILE LISTENING TO FRIENDS AND FAMILY

How can you counsel someone who has gone through a life-changing event about which you have no concept. Yet you may know someone who needs reaching out to.

First you have to clean your own slate. No guilt, blame, shame, or judgment should be made. Next clear your mind of any animosity you may have toward your friend. This will turn to blame when understanding and support are needed. Talk is important, but the person may be reticent, feeling judged or insecure for having such thoughts.

For me it meant that my family did not understand the myriad challenges facing me. Perhaps I was too unsure of myself during my challenges to communicate effectively or reach out for more help. There was a lot that transpired in a short period of time, it was overwhelming enough just to keep sane and keep up with the non stop barrage of crises I had to face. Three years later I believe some of them are beginning relate to what I went through. For myself a physician having gone through such an experience myself helped me understand what the problems are in the recovery period in a whole new different light. It is the mind that needs to heal first or come to terms with what has unfolded before physically the body can recover. Thus Your friend may feel that there's no one on his or her wavelength and feelings of abandonment may surface. . Any advice is misdirected and counterproductive if not sincere and from the heart.

The person may become withdrawn while building up defenses against the incessant barrage of intrusions that seem misguided and maligning. It is absolutely not okay to say, "chin up, eat well exercise, reduce the stress, and everything will be all right."

The person has likely heard this so many times that it sounds grating and condescending. It is said more so that the speaker can reassure himself or herself that he has made a to-ken gesture to cheer the friend on. It is superficial. Give it up. Most cases of cheering up are wrong for that period in time; we do more damage than good. Thus our good friend becomes even more reserved and reticent and blocks you out all the more.

So you have a loved one, for example, who has been laid bare to the bones as far as his respect goes. Probably inappropriately clothed on a hospital bed, all orifices probed and fingered, and every natural body function exposed. Stripped of all humanity, he comes back to his world. What may he have gone through? What experiences may he have had? In a blink of an eye his world has been turned upside down, inside out, dehumanized.

He is not really concerned about this world this minute, yet he is bothered by its intrusions. He may have had a spiritual experience; he may suddenly realize how vulnerable life is and that it can be ended so easily and abruptly. Stability is gone. If he is well after the event and the medical intervention is rather brief and minimally invasive, recovery may be relatively easy, with minimal disruption.

I would imagine the later in life such an event happens and the more settled the person is his one personal life, then the transition back to the living world may go smoother. The more unsettled a person is when such a calamity occurs, the more likely it is that the transition back will be rough.

To empathize with someone, you have to let your guard down and reveal things about yourself that otherwise are buried deeply within. Expose your vulnerabilities; let your friend see the scars of battles you have been through.

Read up on post-traumatic stress disorder, depression, and other related conditions. Look for mood swings, withdrawal, apathy, and excessive emotional states. In my case, these signified impending depression. Indeed I seeked professional counseling for some time. There was mixed feelings in me at the time at how much it helped me, yet looking back it helped me overcome the worse, when there was a time that ending it all would be okay. Fortunately that was brief and therapy effective. Being treated does not mean that the mental challenges will resolve for good. Nope, they likely will recur sporadically with greater or lesser severity. Always take time out to do a self evaluation with your friend, things may even change from day to day.

If further calamities should occur during recovery, look past them and imagine a time when the doom is done. If there seems no good outcome, eventually there will be, it just may not be the one you wanted Visualize the worst and mentally live in the dumpster syndrome, as I call it. I forced myself to do so repeatedly to move beyond the worst-case scenario and keep on strategizing. If you are going to lose possessions, let it happen. It is not worth holding on to. You are only holding on to pain and suffering. The quicker you accept that so much is lost, then you have freed up some of yourself to think positively again.

There is light; look for it. I repeatedly thought all was lost, and yet after each storm there were blue skies and renewed feelings of hope. Be expedient in your changes. Get the necessary help, do the obvious. It will seem so less painless afterward.

At the start of my awakening I thought of the consequences of what had happened to me and how it would affect my family. It was bleak, but certain vicissitudes had to be undertaken to ensure our survival. Luckily I didn't fall into the morass of guilt and paralyzing self-doubt. Perhaps I would still be a miserable chap now. Yet as decisions were made I was freer to move on with my life and make a new start.

The more you hold onto what should have been, could have been, and would have been, the more pain is going on. It is futile. Once I had decided that I could live with all my losses I was in a much better place. There were calmer waters beyond it, and I started thinking constructive thoughts because I had given up a useless fight. For once I actually gave myself valuable advice, though I had to repeat it often to believe in it. It became my daily mantra for a few months and served me well to transition to a place of relative strength.

Hopefully for you,[the friend] by now some skill has been developed to empathize and have a more nonjudgmental attitude. You have learnt to listen to nonsensical ramblings and incoherencies, and stay with it. Even as trust and a deepening bond develop it is time to encourage the rest of the body to awaken again. Physical activity is paramount to recovery. Start with walks on the lawn in sunlight. Do as little as you like, but stick with it. Establish a routine and make it yours and his daily mantra. Do not let your friend quit any activities. Doing something constructive dispels negativity for that length of time. Always encourage your friend to move forward and be there step by step. This shows care, dedication, and solidity. Your friend needs to lean against an oak tree for support. Share his burden. For heart patients I cannot stress enough to get into cardiac rehab. Those folk are invaluable. I built up great confidence in a very a short period.

Exercise does many positive things. Its lasting effects carry way beyond when activity has stopped. Powerful chemicals called endorphins are released that soothe the brain, ease pain, and increase relaxation. Anxiety attacks settle down. The key is consistency. An hour playing golf, learning a new skill indulging an old hobby is one hour spent less in disquiet.

Nutrition is important. Make it work for your friend. Right after hospitalization we need the comfort of a warm fuzzy colorful blanket. Good nutritious food made the right way, and giving up processed foods in place of more wholesome fare will help. Without adequate amounts of complete nutrition, the body will suffer. Recovery will be slower and energy levels lower. I cannot stress enough: do not start any radical dietary changes right away. It will dishearten you. Read up on good food, modify that for your taste, mix it up with exercise and other activities, and you may start to feel better sooner. As his friend, help him make the meals he needs. Variety and experimentation are key. I myself developed a severe obsession for watermelon, chicken salad sandwiches among a few others.

Consider suggesting a new direction in life. Maybe his old job was too stressful, lifestyle too hectic, too many irons in the fire. Are you strong enough to gently try turning the Titanic around, to even suggest it. Adaptation, learning to go slower, taking a new path did it for me. Make the changes gradual or not, Never give up what you'll have until you can truly change direction. Slow down. Material possessions are not important. Give up what was a fantasy. Lots of people are learning to do with much less. We must downsize to grow again. I myself have less, but more of what is important to me, it is more apropos to my new mantra.

20

WHERE AM I NOW?

I had to grow spiritually. It happened of its own volition. No I am not born again, in the traditional sense. I don't do mass more than three times a year. My dialogues were my spiritual bonds. They started in my darkest deepest throes of despair. From raw anger and fear they[my bonds] helped to develop a new version of sanity. I do in the near future want go for yoga and meditation retreats. The wave that has just started has to grow to propel me in this new direction I have chosen. It has done me well so far and will help overcome further negative bad habits.

I would like to join outdoor hiking clubs, and investigate the wonderful Sierra Mountains that surround us. I would like to camp in solitude under a canopy of stars and learn some basic survival skills. I would visit mud baths and hot pools in their natural state, not at some fancy made up lodge.

Hobbies take you away to a dream place. You take a break from reality to a time from the past. My hobbies included re-arranging my music collection, learning to play musical instruments like the drums and now the guitar, and although I'm quite tone deaf, it is pleasing to my ears. My youngest one day told me I sounded better, but he was not sure why. That was high praise indeed, double handed as it may have been.

Join church groups of the support variety. It is good tonic to listen to others who have had similar or worse problems than yours. Talk therapy has its place. I am still friends with some of the people I met. What happened at the meetings stays there, but the camaraderie lingers on. But not everything is for everybody. Find out what rocks your boat the most and stick with it.

Visit the hospital where you were treated. It may give closure to issues bothering you. You may see things you have not seen before. I cherish my interval spent elsewhere; it made me realize there was a huge dimension to human life that we don't see living superficially. But the price was so high to gain more insight that I wonder sometimes was it worth it. I have always been a complicated person, and now I am happy for what I have gone through. I am sorry for the pain I caused myself and my family. I do feel guilty for what they endured because of my circumstances and the conflicts it caused.

Most of all, I do feel sorry for myself. I feel sad that I didn't have time to grieve for myself to let go of feelings that I clung to for too long. I didn't know one grieved for oneself until a co-worker told me about it. How true it sounds. We need to feel sorry for ourselves in a supportive environment before getting strong enough to move on again.

Bluntly I would say that before my MI, my personality was that of a hard-boiled egg: set in its ways. Now it is more of a soft- or half-boiled egg. It has been set by genetics, experiences, and the challenges we place on ourselves in the course of our life. Unfortunately we don't praise ourselves enough for our accomplishments, but rather we beat ourselves up for any real or perceived imperfections. It is a challenge and reward system. Unfortunately we challenge ourselves continuously but don't feel vindicated enough to take rewards. Monetary gain has so surpassed all other forms of creativity in us that we may be altering our genetic code to accept this false reward. In a true reward we give worth to ourselves for our accomplishment. We are our own tooting horn. How often do we go down the less traveled path?

Eighteen months after my incident I traveled to a hot springs destination in a remote part of the Sierras of California. It had unique bathing systems of hot sulphurous waters piped from the earth itself. The trip was simplicity itself, no airports, customs or luggage to haul around. The spring gravity-fed into the individual baths located on site; The bath tubs themselves were carved out of the local rock and two people were to bathe at a given time lending to a more medieval and intimate bathing experience. It was so rustic I could imagine myself back in the Wild West again. At an altitude of nine thousand feet, I was huffing and puffing away from the exertion. In the spa my wife surprised with a massage from an Indian medicine woman. She sensed my unease and that I was troubled by dark waters within. Thus followed an interesting interlude with a session that was physical yet out did the physical. Mystical incantations flowed as emanating from the haunting beauty of the forest at this majestic altitude, and the fragrance of fresh pine and spruce intoxicated the senses and lulled one into a mild narcosis. The food locally prepared was simple yet exquisite on the palate. We were tasting the very environment in which we were staying.

On the sides of the hills around us we followed ancient trails that took us again to crevices and gullies where ran more hot springs, with bubbles of gas coming up from cracks in the rocks under us. The water could only be taken in short intervals because of the intense warmth. I could imagine the water had come in contact with hot rocks somewhere in the crust of the earth and absorbed the essence of the rocks. The water fought its way up under pressure to the cracks between the rocks and allowed us to bathe in its primordial essence.

Because of my physical state, activity was severely limited, rests were frequent and mandatory to catch my breath, yet it was not the quantity yet the quality of what we did that stays with me to this day. Maybe my infirmary let me to take an unhurried pace making me more intimately aware of my surroundings.

Sleep was deep and total after a day filled with simple yet satisfying activities. Morning breakfast cooked on a grill over an open fire never tasted so good. We were not on a beach constantly eating and being served margaritas; nor was it like being in a casino with its hypnotic metallic turns of the machine that took a will of god not to play on.

And as we left that spot as we traveled down the narrow, uneven one-lane road graded with cracked rocks occasionally having to pull off to accommodate other vehicles, We stopped at isolated meadows and gently wandered. The naturalness of the whole place is what I remember the most. Its elegance lay in its simplicity; That simple walk I remember more on than the most fanciful resort I have vacationed in, and I have attended a few some of which are not listed anywhere except by word of mouth.

What was the lesson I took away from this vacation? Life is simplicity itself. We humans always make it more complicated than what it should be. Everything we need is very near, yet we always look for greener pasture elsewhere. That perhaps is built into our genetic code. Didn't our ancient forefathers raid neighboring tribes to steal a bride and whatever else.

What else did I learn? On these vacations I forgot about myself and felt in harmony with the world around me. Letting go is the essence of reinventing and rediscovering who one is.

The change in me had started a few years before my MI after a peculiar incident when I was supposed to talk about some medical condition at my local church. There was a men's support group meeting that evening, and after requesting out of curiosity to join in was allowed to do so. I joined a group of men who were earnestly talking about their feelings. It was an eye-opener to hear grown men talk about deep, intimate issues. I was the shy one then, and yet the fascination to feel that I was not the only one bothered with issues showed me how self-centered I had become. There were people in far dire straits than myself but who showed more concern for their fellow brethren than I ever could. My revelation had already begun, but I could not see it. I was too high and mighty.

I felt bonds develop with several of the men in the meeting and attended again and again. Finally I reached a point where I could speak of things that bothered me, though I was not really sure what really ailed me. I was looking for questions to answers that were already out there.

Eventually I became comfortable, and the seniors asked me to intervene with members who were in deep trouble. I seemed to know something about deep counseling, and coupled with my medical background I manage to reach others. There was a feeling in myself that I had an ability to read others easily. I could sense people in great or grave difficulty. But reticence was difficult to overcome. I found that simply relating my difficulties, even if I didn't get a reply, helped recognition develop so that someone seems to know what the situation is that I am in. I would keep blabbering. The outcome was that a few got the help they desperately needed, and it was such a bonus on the expression of their family that there might be hope after all in their particular dire straits.

This led me to examine what sort of a person I was. My lesson, and the purpose of this book, taught me that when things are the blackest, when hope is all gone, thinking of others suffering worse than me gave me the strength to straighten my perspective, to lighten my own burden, and to find solutions to my own problems. May I call this sharing?

I have learned to say "I'm sorry," and I hope I get better at it. We are right; I read somewhere, less than 50 percent of the time. In our arguments, the same must be true. We need to be sorry because we were wrong. Disarm yourself, show your weakness, and others will open to you. Choose friendships or they will choose you.

I still am trying to unburden myself of all that I have learned. In life we have so many negative experiences; those encounters leave reminders on our hard drives. Every now and then we have to purge those emotional data banks that clutter our mind and destroy any joy we have.

For me, it was to resolve long standing conflicts, to move onto new challenges, to go where I had only ventured in my dreams. Momentum, though, is hard to keep up. One bad week can wreck a month's hard work. I have enjoyed seeing the difference in me as new thoughts and ideas materialize. They are all so positive at this time. After a very long time can I say I have had a productive year, and actually feel some gain has been accomplished.

The following may sound irrational or even more logical. By helping others I find strengths that I never knew I had. I was engrossed in myself and forgot that I lived in a community. On the surface I was enjoying being a wheeler-dealer. Yet it caused a lot of stress and internal damage just waiting to explode. By giving up on this foolishness and having a new lease on life, I'm not sure how, but listening to others has made my friends that much closer. As this cultivates me I feel some good has been done, and that makes me feel good about myself.

I knew my English was good, yet as I write it only gets better. It has filled me with much joy to accomplish this writing and seeing the project come to fruition. If anyone gains any insight from my experiences then it has served its purpose.

For three years I was a frail figure, bent to near breaking like a coconut trunk violently swaying in cyclone winds. But I survived. I look back over that period repeatedly, living its raw intensity on occasion. I am frightened by what happened to me and doubt I would want to live through another such episode. I try to be a stronger role model to my boys again. I hope they and others can look back one day and learn from my experience. And if my boys should have to go through their own crises one day, maybe these thoughts will be of use to them.

I am stronger for revealing my weaknesses, as the light of day only give food to the body and brushes the cobwebs away, and clears the mind of holding onto beliefs that it deems unpleasant only to open us up to fresh material and a higher level of understanding, and moving on rather than stagnating somewhere in our great "circle of life."

Prior to my experience, I had lived to work. Now work is only one facet of my life. During my recovery I learned that this attachment to work was a fundamental defect in my make-up. Yet this is what my training had taught me: to work under extraordinary conditions, beyond the point of exhaustion, and then to try to live a normal life. I was deluding myself, as so many others have already done and continue to do. Sometimes I wonder if we can ever find our original selves again, buried is we are by layers upon layers of life's useless experiences. Cerebrally I am lighter than I've been in a long time. I have to curb my enthusiasm to jump into business ventures again. Simplicity in thought keeps the hard drive less crowded. Just choose activities that make you happy, as I have done with my new hobbies. Yet much is always left to be done. The dark side is ever prevalent like a miasma.

Unburdened by some of the responsibilities of being OCD { obsessive compulsive disorder] at work it has become lighter more fulfilling. Sharing my feelings with others has been a great two-way street. Work less but be more effectively. I hope I can stick to my limitations. We set goals for ourselves and with each goal we meet we raise the bar that much. What is a goal? It is only a target to aim for. Set your goal wherever you want. It does not have to be higher each time. Lower the bar and hit the target. You have reached your goal.

Mentally most of the despair and depression has lifted. I am a quieter person for my experience. Worthless intrusions bother me. But belly shaking laughter with friends from back home lightens my mood. I look back at my worst days, and at times I thought of ending it all.

I have given up business. My hard drive has been cleared of that clutter and is that much faster. I have no regrets. I am confident that if ever I need to, I could turn it on again. Yet it is time to travel down a different path and stay here for some time. I will stay open to new guidance and always welcome new challenges as long as they have a benign intent.

If I was a free spirit tomorrow, unencumbered by work, responsibilities, or a fixed schedule I would like to get on a three-wheeled motorcycle and launch on a gigantic tour of North America. Starting from my hometown, I see me strapping the missus down in the captain's chair. I'd cruise north through Nevada, Utah, and Idaho, cross the border and continue through the great Canadian forests to Yellowknife, near the Arctic Circle (read ice road truckers). Having had my fill of the Arctic summer, we'd head southeast through the prairies of central Canada, stopping at Calgary and Edmonton, visiting with friends we haven't seen in decades. We'd continue east to Toronto, visit with my wife's sisters and extended family, and eat the my fill of the best Indian and Paki food outside of those countries. Maybe my brothers-in-law would take me to those clubs where they have a pole surrounded by mirrors. Continuing on my tour, we'd head south into the States, racing down the East Coast, taking our sweet time at every town we find, visiting again with friends and family. Hanging west from Florida we'd explore Cajun country, eat jambalaya, steamed crawdads, greens and fried chicken, Andouille sausage and shrimp etouffe, corn bread and sweet potato pie, and check myself into a cardiac center. After all that food, I'd be looking for trouble.

Maybe I'd like to quit working in one place and do a *locum tenens* type job, enjoying different parts of the country while working temporary assignments. Our small town does not offer much, but it has got me this far.

Writing this book has been as valuable as anything else in helping me overcome my issues. I am proud to put a few words to paper that have made some sense. Perhaps I'd like to visit Pakistan soon and write of my experience growing up in that country. There will be so many twists and turns and contradictions to get my story out, though, I fear it may get too technical. Yet this may be a worthy challenge and one worth undertaking.

The view Westerners have of the other half of the world is what has been fed to them by the press and our governments. One can find the same issues with religion and race in all countries. I have lived on both sides of the world. There is another viewpoint to the crises we are living in today. It is more important to get along than to be right. For in the final judgment, who knows what is right? We all sin in so many ways, but we only put our best foot forward, showing our good side only.

I know this: the more I know, the less smart I become. The complexity of life and thought is beyond me. I am but a grain of sand in this world. Am I really smarter or wiser for my experience, or just deluded?

Physically, I have come a long way since I needed my wife's assistance to take a shower and needing a water pill to get the extra fluid out of my lungs. Today I can do a two-hour work-out at the gym with gaps and recovery days. Recently I cycled twenty miles nonstop. Then I was out for three days, but it was worth it. It is important to me to mention these physical landmarks; they are some of the indicators I have that all is well, and they give me some hope that I will not have another cardiac event soon.

On some website you punch in all your medical data and it tells you what your life expectancy. My life expectancy is 62.7 years. At this writing, I have about 10.6 years left to live, according to this model. Talk about making the best of what one has.

I will continue to meet new physical challenges, perhaps some hikes in the high country of Yosemite National Park. I think my friend will be waiting for me around a hidden bend, or he'll leave evidence of his presence in my path. For it is time to talk to again, and much needs to be said.

Addendum

AS RELATED BY WAYNE CASTELLINO

March 23, 2012.

Four years and twenty days after the initial event.

My father was hospitalized at Fresno Heart. He was experiencing a tad swelling on his shins and a lack of endurance in his workouts.

An angiogram was done which showed recurrent blockage at the initial location spread over two sites close to each other. Two stents were placed. His Heart function is now at fifteen percent. Walking one hundred yards leaves him winded. He has not given up and will start on his recovery program very shortly. Discouraged he is yes, defeated he is not and tells me he will go down swinging or will find ways to beat it again. Being a realist he understands the paradigm has changed again.

His utmost goal as he related to me just as he was wheeled into the surgical suite is to see his us, his sons settled and Doreen taken care of before he ponders the inescapable.